PSYCHO-SPIRITUAL THERAPY

Jacquelyne Morison

Jacquelyne Morison Publishing

All material © Jacquelyne Morison 2019 unless otherwise stated. The right of Jacquelyne Morison to be identified as the author of this work has been asserted by her in accordance with the Copyright, Designs and Patents Act 1988.

All rights reserved. Except as permitted under current legislation no part of this work may be photocopied, stored in a retrieval system, published, performed in public, adapted, broadcast, transmitted, recorded or reproduced in any form or by any means without the prior permission of the copyright owner. All enquiries should be addressed to Jacquelyne Morison Publishing.

British Library of Cataloguing-in-Publication Data

A catalogue entry for this book is available from the British Library.

ISBN 978-0-9929973-5-9

Published in Cheltenham by Jacquelyne Morison Publishing 2019.

CONTENTS

PSYCHO-SPIRITUAL THERAPY — 1

Psycho-Spiritual Therapy Practice — 3
What is psycho-spiritual therapy? — 3
Healing practice — 3
Character analysis practice — 4
Psycho-spiritual therapy assignments — 4

Psycho-Spiritual Therapy Origin — 6
What is the origin of psycho-spiritual therapy? — 6
Analytical psychology — 6
Transpersonal psychology — 6
Psychosynthesis — 7
Core-process psychotherapy — 7

NATURAL LAW — 9

Natural Law Practice — 11
What is natural law? — 11

Life Law — 12
What is the natural law of life? — 12
Attraction — 12
Projection — 13
Attachment — 13
Reflection — 13
Request — 14
Cause and effect — 14
Natural law of life therapeutic text — 14

Creation Law — 17
What is the natural law of creation? — 17
Flow — 17
Abundance — 18
Clarity — 18
Intention — 18

Manifestation	19
Natural law of creation therapeutic text	19

HIGHER AWARENESS LAW **21**
What is the natural law of higher awareness?	21
Balance	21
Karma	22
Discernment	22
Affirmation	22
Meditation	22
Challenge	23
Natural law of higher awareness therapeutic text	23

HIGHER FREQUENCY LAW **25**
What is the natural law of higher frequency?	25
Vibration	25
Purification	25
Perspective	26
Gratitude	26
Grace	26
Natural law of higher frequency therapeutic text	27

SUCCESS LAW **28**
What is the natural law of success?	28
Potential	28
Generosity	28
Effort	29
Desire	29
Detachment	29
Obligation	29
Natural law of success therapeutic text	30

ENERGETIC HEALING   **33**

ENERGETIC HEALING PRACTICE **35**
What is energetic healing?	35
Spiritual healing practice	35
Meditative practice	36
Psychotherapeutic practice	36
Alternative therapeutic practice	36

ENERGETIC FIELDS **37**
What is an energetic field?	37
Etheric field	38

Mental field	38
Astral field	39
Energetic fields therapeutic text	40

CHAKRA HEALING — 43

CHAKRA HEALING PRACTICE — 45
What is chakra healing? — 45

LOWER CHAKRA SYSTEM — 47
What is the lower chakra system? — 47
Root chakra — 48
Sacral chakra — 48
Solar plexus — 49
Heart chakra — 49
Throat chakra — 50
Brow chakra — 50
Crown chakra — 51
Lower chakra system therapeutic text — 51

HIGHER CHAKRA SYSTEM — 55
What is the higher chakra system? — 55
Higher self chakra — 56
Soul wisdom chakra — 56
Synchronicity chakra — 57
Soul journey chakra — 57
Cosmic connection chakra — 57
Higher chakra system therapeutic text — 58

AGE-REGRESSION — 60
What is age-regression? — 60
Age-regression therapeutic text — 60

PAST-LIFE REGRESSION — 63
What is past-life regression? — 63
Past-life regression therapeutic text — 63

ANGELIC HEALING — 67

ANGELIC HEALING PRACTICE — 69
What is angelic healing? — 69

GUARDIAN ANGELS — 71
What is a guardian angel? — 71
Guardian angels therapeutic text — 71

ARCHANGELS 73
- What is an archangel? 73
- Uriel 74
- Gabriel 74
- Jophiel 74
- Raphael 74
- Chamuel 74
- Michael 74
- Raziel 75
- Zadkiel 75
- Haniel 75
- Metatron 75
- Energetic healing links to angelic healing 75
- Archangels therapeutic text 76

ASCENDED MASTERS 79
- What is an ascended master? 79
- El Morya Khan 80
- Lord Lanto 80
- Paul the Venetian 80
- Serapis Bay 80
- Hilarion 81
- Lady Nada 81
- Saint Germain 81
- Ascended masters therapeutic text 81

LORDS OF KARMA 83
- What is a lord of karma? 83
- Great divine director 84
- Goddess of liberty 84
- Lady Nada 84
- Pallas Athena 85
- Cyclopea 85
- Kwan Yin 85
- Lady Portia 85
- Lords of karma therapeutic text 85

SHAMANIC HEALING 89

SHAMANIC HEALING PRACTICE 91
- What is shamanic healing? 91

SHAMANIC JOURNEYING 92
- What is shamanic journeying? 92

Shamanic guides and teachers	93
Eagle	94
Bear	94
Wolf	94
Buffalo	94
Shamanic journeying therapeutic text	94

Shamanic Soul Retrieval ... 96
What is shamanic soul retrieval? ... 96
Shamanic soul retrieval therapeutic text ... 96

TAROT   99

Tarot Practice ... 101
What is tarot? ... 101

Major Arcana ... 102
What is the major arcana? ... 102
Major arcana therapeutic text ... 104

Minor Arcana ... 107
What is the minor arcana? ... 107
Rods ... 108
Pentacles ... 108
Swords ... 109
Cups ... 109
Minor arcana standard cards ... 109
Minor arcana court cards ... 110
Minor arcana therapeutic text ... 111

ASTROLOGY   115

Astrological Practice ... 117
What is astrology? ... 117

Exoteric-Esoteric Astrology ... 119
What is exoteric-esoteric astrology? ... 119
Exoteric astrology ... 119
Esoteric astrology ... 120
Exoteric-esoteric astrology therapeutic tasks ... 121

Zodiac Signs ... 122
What is a zodiac sign? ... 122
Zodiac sign numbers ... 123
Zodiac sign elements ... 124

Zodiac sign qualities 125
Zodiac sign genders 126
Angelic healing links to astrology 127
Tarot links to astrology 129
Zodiac signs therapeutic tasks 130

PLANETARY SIGNS 131
What is a planetary sign? 131
Inner planets 132
Outer planets 132
Exoteric-esoteric planets 133
Planetary signs therapeutic tasks 134

ASTROLOGICAL HOUSES 135
What is an astrological house? 135
Astrological house numbers 135
Astrological house modes 137
Astrological houses therapeutic tasks 138

SIGN-PLANET-HOUSE CONFIGURATION 139
What is a sign-planet-house configuration? 139
Aries-first house 139
Taurus-second house 140
Gemini-third house 140
Cancer-fourth house 141
Leo-fifth house 142
Virgo-sixth house 142
Libra-seventh house 143
Scorpio-eighth house 143
Sagittarius-ninth house 144
Capricorn-tenth house 145
Aquarius-eleventh house 145
Pisces-twelfth house 146
Sign-planet-house configuration therapeutic tasks 146

ASTROLOGICAL AXES 148
What is an astrological axis? 148
Opposing zodiac signs 148
Ascendant and descendant axis 149
Imum coeli and medium coeli axis 150
South node and north node axis 151
Hemispheres 152
Quadrants 153
Astrological axes therapeutic tasks 154

Natal Chart 156
What is a natal chart? 156
Natal chart interpretation 158
Natal chart axes 159
Natal chart sign elements 160
Natal chart sign qualities 161
Natal chart sign genders 162
Natal chart house modes 163
Natal chart hemispheres 164
Natal chart quadrants 165
Natal chart therapeutic tasks 166

NUMEROLOGY   167

Numerological Practice 169
What is numerology? 169

Life Path Numbers 170
What is a life path number? 170
Life path number calculation 170
Life path number attributes 171
Leader 172
Mediator 172
Socialite 172
Worker 172
Freedom lover 172
Peace lover 172
Thinker 173
Manager 173
Teacher 173
Giver 173
Master builder 173
Master healer 174
Angelic healing links to life path numbers 174
Astrological links to life path numbers 175
Life path number therapeutic tasks 176

Soul Expression Numbers 177
What is a soul expression number? 177
Soul expression number calculation 177
Soul expression number example 178
Soul expression number attributes 178
Soul expression number therapeutic tasks 179

Soul Urge Numbers 180
- What is a soul urge number? 180
- Soul urge number calculation 180
- Soul urge number example 181
- Soul urge number attributes 181
- Soul urge number therapeutic tasks 182

Personality Numbers 183
- What is a personality number? 183
- Personality number calculation 183
- Personality number example 184
- Personality number attributes 184
- Personality number therapeutic tasks 185

Personal Year Numbers 186
- What is a personal year number? 186
- Personal year number calculation 186
- Personal year number attributes 186
- Personal year number therapeutic tasks 187

Birth Day Numbers 188
- What is a birth day number? 188
- Birth day number calculation 188
- Birth day number attributes 188
- Birth day number therapeutic tasks 190

HEALING RAYS — 191

Healing Ray Practice 193
- What is a healing ray? 193

Healing Ray Life Path 194
- What is a healing ray life path? 194
- Blue ray 195
- Yellow ray 195
- Pink ray 195
- White ray 196
- Green ray 196
- Purple ray 196
- Violet ray 196
- Energetic healing links to healing rays 196
- Angelic healing links to healing rays 197
- Astrological links to healing rays 198
- Healing rays therapeutic tasks 199

APPENDICES 201

FURTHER READING 203
INDEX 205
ABOUT JACQUELYNE MORISON 207

Psycho-Spiritual Therapy

PSYCHO-SPIRITUAL THERAPY

The value of psycho-spiritual therapy will be to allow you to select those healing routes which will be particularly appropriate for you.

Psycho-spiritual therapy will enable you to resolve your pain and suffering and to understand yourself at a deep level.

PSYCHO-SPIRITUAL THERAPY PRACTICE

What is psycho-spiritual therapy?

Psycho-spiritual therapy is a distillation of therapeutic approaches and archetypal symbolism for character analysis which collectively form a synthesis of tools for you to heal your soul.

Psycho-spiritual therapeutic intervention essentially embodies meditative and metaphysical healing practice, which utilises your inner mind rather than your intellect, yet combines this practice with psychotherapeutic methodology as a talking cure.

The pure scientists believe that humankind serves no tangible or meaningful purpose but has simply evolved by chance many centuries ago because human life could be sustained on the earthly planet. Metaphysical doctrine, however, will provide you with a means of understanding the purpose of life and those who are clairvoyant, clairaudient and/or clairsentient have offered experiential evidence that there is indeed a cosmic plan and part of this purpose will be your self-healing journey.

You can regard the contents of *Psycho-Spiritual Therapy* and metaphysical philosophy generally, however, as having principally a symbolic therapeutic value rather than having a literal meaning according to your personal belief inclinations. If you find your belief systems challenged with certain controversial issues, consequently, then merely take the essence of what you are reading and adapt it freely to suit your own requirements.

Healing practice

Psycho-spiritual therapeutic intervention will essentially embrace various energetic healing practices which will involve both physical healing and imaginative mind-oriented healing.

Psycho-Spiritual Therapy has, consequently, included accepted healing practices in the guise of energetic healing, chakra healing, angelic healing and shamanic healing. Other healing practices, such as vortex healing, reiki healing, colour healing, crystal healing and music-sound healing, can equally be included under the umbrella of psycho-spiritual therapy if these practices are familiar and appropriate for you.

Imaginative healing practices in the form of creative visualisation, guided meditation, hypnotic age-regression and hypnotic past-life regression can also be included under the umbrella of psycho-spiritual therapeutic practice.

CHARACTER ANALYSIS PRACTICE

An important aspect of psycho-spiritual therapy will be the nature of character analysis which will be inherent within various divinatory practices. This form of character analysis will embody powerful archetypal symbolism which can bring about profound healing change for you – particularly when combined with other healing modalities.

Natural law, in itself, can also strongly argue the case further for including the symbolic facets of divinatory practices within the compass of psycho-spiritual therapy.

Divination methodology which embraces predictive methodology will be, however, outside the scope of this book because psycho-spiritual therapy is primarily a healing medium. *Psycho-Spiritual Therapy* will, therefore, only consider tarot, astrology, numerology and the healing rays as a powerful means of exploring your soul and its evolutionary purpose rather than incorporating any predictive methodology.

PSYCHO-SPIRITUAL THERAPY ASSIGNMENTS

At the end of each section of *Psycho-Spiritual Therapy* you will find a number of practical therapeutic assignments. These therapeutic assignments will cover both therapeutic texts which can be employed for self-hypnosis, therapeutic relaxation, guided meditation and creative visualisation and therapeutic tasks which can be used for contemplating your character traits and identifying your life's mission.

You can utilise the assignments which have been included within *Psycho-Spiritual Therapy* either with the aid of a qualified professional practitioner or you can work on these projects yourself with a trusted friend. You will, in most cases, be able to undertake the assignments in *Psycho-Spiritual*

Therapy unaided but, if this ploy fails, then you would be strongly advised to seek professional assistance from a psycho-spiritual therapeutic practitioner.

Ask a trusted friend to read each hypnotic practice text contained within this book to you very slowly or record these texts yourself in order to play them back to yourself when appropriate. You can, of course, freely adapt these therapeutic texts in order to suit your own unique requirements or your personal circumstances.

It should be emphasized to the reader that regular meditative practice, creative visualisation and self-hypnosis alone will be largely insufficient for effective healing and will certainly be no substitute for therapeutic intervention with a qualified professional practitioner. You would be advised, consequently, to utilise the wisdom and the assignments which have been included within *Psycho-Spiritual Therapy* in conjunction with therapeutic work undertaken with your chosen psycho-spiritual therapeutic practitioner rather than using this book as an all-embracing panacea for all your ills.

PSYCHO-SPIRITUAL THERAPY ORIGIN

WHAT IS THE ORIGIN OF PSYCHO-SPIRITUAL THERAPY?

Psycho-spiritual therapy must surely have its origins in antiquity but for the purpose of simplicity you can assume that the practice began ostensibly more recently with the work of psychodynamic, humanistic and transpersonal psychotherapy pioneers (see Figure 1: *Psycho-Spiritual Therapy Origins*).

FIGURE 1: PSYCHO-SPIRITUAL THERAPY ORIGINS

ANALYTICAL PSYCHOLOGY	TRANSPERSONAL PSYCHOLOGY	PSYCHOSYNTHESIS	CORE-PROCESS PSYCHOTHERAPY
Carl Jung	Ken Wilber Roger Walsh Frances Vaughan	Roberto Assagioli	Maura Sills

ANALYTICAL PSYCHOLOGY

Analytical Psychology was devised by Carl Jung (1875-1961) who hailed from the psychoanalytic tradition of Sigmund Freud (1856-1939) but he also steered his clinical practice towards a metaphysical approach and thereby set up a trend for the future.

Analytical Psychology will advocate therapeutic intervention which highlights archetypal imagery, dream symbolism, spiritual guidance and transcendence as part of your progressive therapeutic journey towards self-fulfilment and the realisation of your true potential.

TRANSPERSONAL PSYCHOLOGY

The so-called fourth school of psychotherapy has generated Transpersonal Psychology which has emanated from the work of Ken Wilber, Roger Walsh, Frances Vaughan, John Battista, Michael Washburn and Stanislav Grof together with several other contributors.

Transpersonal Psychology will be important because it is essentially an integrative practice which will encourage wholeness and human growth.

Transpersonal Psychology encompasses psychodynamic and humanistic ideals with a view to your healing transformation by focusing on individuation goals, mindfulness, spiritual awareness, self-potential realisation and compassion towards others.

Psychosynthesis

Psychosynthesis was essentially the brainchild of Roberto Assagioli (1888-1974) who recognised the fact that your innermost thoughts are reflected in your perception of the outer world.

Psychosynthesis will acknowledge that you may be subject to possessing a number of negative sub-personalities which can come into play unexpectedly and can cause havoc within you as a result. Psychosynthesis, therefore, will endeavour to heal those fragmented parts of your soul which have resulted from untoward life experiences.

Core-process psychotherapy

Core-Process Psychotherapy was formulated by Maura Sills as her means of combining psychodynamic practice with mindfulness and Buddhist doctrine.

Core-Process Psychotherapy will consider the psychodynamics of the relationship between you and your therapeutic practitioner as a means of empowering you to make important realisations about yourself and your significant others in the therapeutic context.

Natural Law

> **NATURAL LAW**
>
> *The value of natural law in the healing context will be to allow you to understand the way in which the social world naturally operates.*
>
> *Natural law will enable you to work within any constraints which society might impose on you and will empower you to be true to yourself.*

NATURAL LAW PRACTICE

Do you realise that natural law governs you, your life and your social interaction?

Do you appreciate that the natural law of the cosmos has evolved because of its inhabitants and their interaction?

Can you envisage your place in the world about you?

WHAT IS NATURAL LAW?

Natural law (or universal law) is an accepted set of principles by which humankind is governed in order to permit humans to live together peacefully and in a spirit of co-operation (see Figure 2: *Natural Law*).

There are an infinite number of natural laws because humankind has inhabited the planet for many centuries but those which will apply to you and your healing voyage can generally be summarised as the key principles of living.

You will discover that the more you undertake your healing journey the more these natural laws will make sense and will automatically apply in your life without your having to force yourself to behave in a prescribed manner.

FIGURE 2: NATURAL LAW

LIFE	CREATION	HIGHER AWARENESS	HIGHER FREQUENCY	SUCCESS

LIFE LAW

Do you find that your emotive responses to others are uncontrollable?

Might you notice that your emotive reactions occur spontaneously and then cause you much distress?

Are you beset by a feeling of inadequacy when it comes to fulfilling your own needs?

WHAT IS THE NATURAL LAW OF LIFE?

The natural law of life will consider the way in which you interact with others and your relationship with yourself (see Figure 3: *Natural Laws of Life*).

The reason why the natural law of life exists is because humankind is a pack-animal species which requires social interaction in order to survive. As a child you will grow up under the umbrella guidance of your parents, your guardians and your educators and this experience will have an unavoidable effect of your unconscious responses and your opinion of yourself in both childhood and adulthood.

The natural law of life will, therefore, assist you to relate to yourself and to others.

FIGURE 3: NATURAL LAWS OF LIFE

ATTRACTION	PROJECTION	ATTACHMENT	REFLECTION	REQUEST	CAUSE & EFFECT

ATTRACTION

The natural law of attraction states that you will attract into your life favourable or unfavourable people and factors according to your need to grow spiritually.

The law of attraction will, therefore, propel you towards the source of your unresolved dilemmas in order to allow you to develop personally. You might, for instance, meet someone or encounter a situation from which you will learn about yourself. Your connection may be welcomed or disastrous but your experience of learning will be beneficial and might not be attained in any other way.

Projection

The natural law of projection states that you will observe traits in others which will actually apply to you.

The law of projection will, therefore, enable you to uncover secrets about yourself which are housed within your inner mind. You might, for instance, see praiseworthy traits in another which you do not have the confidence to acknowledge in yourself or you may accuse another unjustifiably of possessing negative characteristics which you might consider to be unacceptable about yourself.

Attachment

The natural law of attachment states that you will have a need to bond with another with whom you share a commonality or a tendency to become attached to material possessions and a given way of life.

The law of attachment will, therefore, allow you to understand your unconscious and uncontrollable motivation with a view to altering your negative inclinations. You might, for instance, be involved with a life partner, a friend or a business associate who will remind you of a parent or a guardian from your childhood. The motivation for your gravitation towards others will, of course, be based on your life experience which may be favourable or unfavourable. You may also give more importance to material items than is perhaps healthy for you as an unconscious and deceptive ploy in order to give yourself the illusion of feeling safe.

Reflection

The natural law of reflection states that you will need to think before you act because you will be the author of the consequences of your own action.

The law of reflection will, therefore, permit you to hold back prior to making an unwise decision or before giving an inappropriate response. You might, for instance, need to wait before making an ill-considered and irrevocable decision about your future or before engaging in conflict with another which would destroy your relationship with that individual.

REQUEST

The natural law of request states that you will need to ask for those things which you require rather than assuming that others can read your mind in order to serve your needs.

The law of request will, therefore, encourage you to have confidence in your own self-worth and not to rely on the opinions of others in order to make you feel better about yourself. You might, for instance, need to ask an intimate partner to consider you in some way or not to take you for granted because this healthy stance will constitute the terms of a successful relationship.

CAUSE AND EFFECT

The natural law of cause and effect states that everything which happens to you does so for a reason because there will be an underlying cause which in turn will control the outcome.

The law of cause and effect will, therefore, enable you to realise that virtually everything in your life happens for a reason. You might, for instance, be motivated to select a life partner or to choose a given career path according to the relationship which your parents or your guardians adopted or the occupation which one of your childhood carers undertook.

NATURAL LAW OF LIFE THERAPEUTIC TEXT

Relax deeply before you embark on the next stage of your healing journey. Give yourself time and space in order to enter the recesses of your inner mind and to find a place which feels safe, warm and comfortable.

Consider carefully your relationship with yourself and those about you both in the present and in the past.

Do you feel that you need to cling to others in order to feel safe and secure?

Or do you feel compelled to reach out to others because you do not feel self-sufficient or you believe that you are inadequate in some way?

Reflect on your attachments and whether they are helpful or unhelpful to you and consider those people to whom you are uncannily attracted yet you do not know why.

Perhaps you can notice some unnatural hooks which you feel link you to someone whom you would actually like to distance yourself from or even to shun in order to free yourself?

Can you then take an oversized pair of scissors and cut those ties which you feel bind you unnecessarily to an alien or an unwanted associate?

Just watch yourself gaining freedom as you imagine cutting the cords which bind and severing the ties which somehow dictate your actions.

Consider those people whom you feel are unkind or hurtful towards you.

Perhaps someone close is inconsiderate or selfish and, therefore, does not acknowledge you as a person or does not cater adequately for your needs?

Can you identify any false friends in your world?

Can you name an intimate partner or a so-called friend who actually does not work in your own interests?

Can you clearly see the situation which is distressing you and yet you feel powerless to address?

Consider those people whom you feel you want to blame because of your own perceived inadequacies and allow yourself to see things realistically as your means of telling it like it is and not as you imagine it to be.

Now will be time to rectify the discrepancies in your life by cutting out the dead wood or telling others how you feel.

Imagine yourself seeing a partner or a relative more realistically and attributing blame where it truly belongs. Stand up for your rights and your wishes and express these thoughts to those about you rather than allowing ideas to fester inside so that you feel upset as a result.

Consider whether your requested needs are met by those closest to you. But pause a while before you take any decisive and irrevocable action.

Take some time out now to consider your relationship with your parents and the relationship which your parents or your guardians formed as their union.

Was there disharmony in your childhood or did you feel unloved?

Was there conflict in your childhood household or was your home torn apart by disruption and hardship?

Often you will find that if you are exposed to relationship disharmony at a young age then, of course, this pattern will seem to be replicated in later life because you will have no blueprint for choosing an appropriate life partner. The cause may go a long way back but you will meet it as the effect in today's life.

Allow all these thoughts to permeate your mind and permit your self-healing capacity to take charge and to assist you for your greatest benefit.

You possess all the knowledge which you will need to take yourself forward and to rectify any situation which can be retrieved successfully. If you feel that a given relationship has run its course then it may be time for you to sever that connection in order to allow yourself to flourish, blossom and grow.

Let all these thoughts settle and know that the right path for you will be chosen in due course by your powerful inner mind.

Now come back slowly and gently to the present moment when you believe that you have truly done everything you can for yourself here and now. And when returning to full conscious awareness congratulate yourself on your achievements and your ability to untangle the negativity of your past.

CREATION LAW

Do you feel that you are out of step with the rest of humanity?

Might you feel deprived of love, safety and security?

Are you aware that your mind is clouded with junk and your life is filled with disaster?

WHAT IS THE NATURAL LAW OF CREATION?

The natural law of creation will consider the way in which you manifest and retain material possessions and spiritual wealth in order to ensure your personal security and your peace of mind (see Figure 4: *Natural Laws of Creation*).

The reason why the natural law of creation exists is because you will be required to create a functional life for yourself within your family and in society.

The natural law of creation will, therefore, assist you to relate to your personal security and your inner contentment.

FIGURE 4: NATURAL LAWS OF CREATION

FLOW	ABUNDANCE	CLARITY	INTENTION	MANIFESTATION

FLOW

The natural law of flow states that you will need to follow the natural course of life and not interfere too much with events, circumstances and the motivation of others.

The law of flow will, therefore, permit you to travel the middle course in life and not seek to over-manipulate others or to radically control a situation in order to accommodate your own needs. You might, for instance, be tempted to alter the character or the actions of another in order to suit your personal requirements. This tendency will not normally be productive for any length of time and will, of course, rob others of their integrity.

Abundance

The natural law of abundance states that you can manifest your requirements without too much effort and without having to manipulate others.

The law of abundance will, therefore, enable you to appreciate your own self-worth and not feel that you are somehow undeserving of wealth or privilege. You might, for instance, feel that you have a right to be satisfied and then demand your rights aggressively which will only result in the suffering and the consequent alienation of others. You might, however, feel that you are somehow unworthy or undeserving of privileges and so you will neglect to take up a genuine offer or to seize an opportunity which would be beneficial for you.

Clarity

The natural law of clarity states that you can see life realistically and in perspective when you undertake your healing mission and when you can divorce yourself from negative thinking.

The law of clarity will, therefore, permit you to regard circumstances realistically and to gauge the negative behaviour of others when you have been ill-treated by someone else rather than justifying the actions of another in order to put yourself in the wrong. You might, for instance, fail to achieve a realistic outlook on life because you are unhealthily attached to people or to possessions and so you seek to excuse the unacceptable behaviour of others close to you.

Intention

The natural law of intention states that you will succeed if your intention towards other individuals is kindly and genuine.

The law of intention will, therefore, encourage you to act from a standpoint of consideration for others without robbing yourself of your own integrity. You might, for instance, feel that you can actually aid someone by helping them to appreciate a harsh lesson in life when your intention is for the highest good of that person rather than being to satisfy your own personal needs.

Manifestation

The natural law of manifestation states that you can effortlessly obtain those things which you desire and deserve in life.

The law of manifestation will, therefore, allow you to strive to create a safe and secure environment for yourself and your family. You might, for instance, imagine that being rich and famous would bring you happiness but this manifestation would come at a price which you might not be prepared to pay. Those things which can genuinely be obtained, however, will be readily available to you.

Natural law of creation therapeutic text

Allow yourself to imagine that you can see a bird flying high in the sky enjoying the brilliance of the sun and the coolness of the breeze.

Could you see yourself as that bird free of burden and restriction and able to lead a carefree life?

Your bird will be able to travel effortlessly on the air currents and can be carried along by the wind across many continents. Your bird simply goes with the flow and yet your bird is free and uninhibited.

Your bird can also enjoy the beauty of his/her surroundings and can observe the world from a great distance and can see things clearly as a result.

Your bird will, however, not be afraid to move forward or to seek opportunities which come his/her way. Your bird believes that he/she is worthy and deserving and, therefore, sees the world as a place of bounty and abundance.

Your bird is able to take from the world those things which he/she wishes for because he/she feels capable of manifesting anything which will serve his/her needs for survival. Your bird can find food and new territories in which to build a nest with a mate so that he/she can rear little birds.

Your bird is simply determined to serve his/her own needs and those of other creatures in the world and in the skies. Your bird will help his/her mate to build the nest and care for the little ones. Your bird will feed his/her little ones and protect them until it will be time for each one to fly from the nest in order to gain his/her own freedom.

Your bird can clearly see all around him/her at those aspects of nature of which other creatures may not be aware because their perspective on life is tainted and unclear. Your bird, therefore, has acquired the gift of clarity and insight.

Now take all these lessons which you have learned today from being a bird and make them your own because you deserve to learn lessons in connection with your healing journey. You will find that all you have learned today will be carried with you forever more and cannot be taken from you by anyone else in the world.

And when you are ready simply drift back to the present moment in order to continue the business of the day enriched by your insights and your experience.

HIGHER AWARENESS LAW

Are you beset by feelings of constant confusion and uncertainty?

Do you find that you do not give yourself enough personal attention when you feel you have heavy responsibilities?

Can you appreciate that misfortune can be overcome and can yield a beneficial and worthwhile result?

WHAT IS THE NATURAL LAW OF HIGHER AWARENESS?

The natural law of higher awareness will consider the way in which you undertake your spiritual journey and you relate to your life's challenges (see Figure 5: *Natural Laws of Higher Awareness*).

The reason why the natural law of higher awareness exists is because you are capable of exploring your own mind and maturing into an independent and free-thinking individual in your own right.

The natural law of higher awareness will, therefore, assist you to relate to your unique healing journey.

FIGURE 5: NATURAL LAWS OF HIGHER AWARENESS

BALANCE	KARMA	DISCERNMENT	AFFIRMATION	MEDITATION	CHALLENGE

BALANCE

The natural law of balance states that you can strive to achieve balance in your life in order to avoid extremes.

The law of balance will, therefore, allow you tread the middle path as your means of keeping within sensible limits. You might, for instance, overreact or fail to respond in a given situation which will inevitably place you at a disadvantage. You may be over-confident about the success of a project on which you embark or you could lack confidence with the result that your undertaking will founder.

Karma

The natural law of karma states that you will need to resolve the negative effects of your own experiences and actions.

The law of karma will, therefore, provide you with an opportunity to resolve the negative aspects of your past experience and to blossom out of any misfortune. You might, for instance, do something or fail to do something which you later regret bitterly but you might actually need to appreciate that this action was your natural response in certain circumstances which were beyond your control.

Discernment

The natural law of discernment states that you can learn to estimate the actions and inactions of others and to draw your own conclusions accurately as a free-standing individual.

The law of discernment, therefore, will be your means of being true to yourself and making your own choices about yourself and your existence. You might, for instance, evaluate a given situation and see it clearly in perspective despite forceful opinions and pressures from others.

Affirmation

The natural law of affirmation states that you can empower yourself with positive thoughts, actions and self-talk and thus relinquish negative thoughts and habits simultaneously.

The law of affirmation will, therefore, empower you to help yourself in a positive manner and to release yourself from negative ties and unhelpful thinking. You might, for instance, use a positive affirmation in order to help yourself to build confidence or to avoid unprofitable temptation once you have resolved the root cause of any dilemma from which you have previously suffered.

Meditation

The natural law of meditation states that you can explore your inner mind with self-hypnosis and with quiet reflection usually as an adjunct to therapeutic assistance.

The law of meditation will, therefore, invite you to seek peace and relaxation and to undertake problem-solving activity. You might, for instance, use daily meditative practice or creative visualisation as a way of bringing yourself peace or relaxing as a means of self-healing when you reside in a hectic world.

CHALLENGE

The natural law of challenge states that you will be presented with obstacles which you will need to overcome in your life so that you can profit from surmounting a negative experience.

The law of challenge will, therefore, permit you to grow spiritually as a result of negative experiences which you can manage to surmount in the interests of human survival. You might, for instance, discover that an unfruitful relationship will, once terminated or resolved, result in a valuable lesson in life for you and will stand you in your stead for the future.

NATURAL LAW OF HIGHER AWARENESS THERAPEUTIC TEXT

> *Let yourself today explore your own mind and further your unique healing journey in this way. Initially you might wish to make yourself comfortable and to lie back and enjoy the ride.*
>
> *Now think about those things within your psyche which are out of balance and somehow just not the way you would like them to be.*
>
> *Look at the anomalies and the contradictions in your life and note the way in which you are affected. Reflect on the polarities and the extremes within your thinking and your actions.*
>
> *Do you find yourself going over the top in some areas and then underplaying in others?*
>
> *Are you effusive and enthusiastic one moment and inexplicably then down in the dumps the next instant?*
>
> *Are you fearful of life sometimes and yet very confident on other occasions?*
>
> *Do you feel cross and angry with certain people and yet calm and accepting of others?*
>
> *Notice all these things about yourself and reflect honestly on what is in your inner mind.*

Can you find a creative way to attain a balance in your life by eradicating the contradictions and the extremes?

Can you find a useful way of putting things right by considering your past experiences?

Can you apportion blame where it is due and not make excuses for other people who have ill-treated you?

Allow yourself to find a way of achieving a balance in your mind rather than harbouring an extreme of over-reaction or under-reaction.

Everything which has happened to you in life will have an inevitable consequence and will affect you deeply. Your action or inaction will inevitably reveal a result of which you may or may not approve.

If you feel fear and anxiety frequently then ask yourself where was the birthplace of this feeling and find a way of reconciling your dreads and trepidation?

Spend some time meditating on these notions.

If you are prone to becoming angry and enraged far too often can you consider who or what in your early life caused you to be cross and justifiably annoyed and then work on seeing your past realistically in order to resolve it satisfactorily?

Allot yourself time for quiet contemplation of your past experiences. Do not make too many excuses for the negative actions of others.

If you feel sad and lonely on many occasions even when you are in a crowd can you identify when and where you first felt this feeling and then comfort yourself in some way?

Give yourself permission to explore your mind here in this moment.

All your distressing feelings will have an origin in your past and will arise in the present as unpleasant manifestations which you can easily resolve. The challenges of the past will permit you to grow and to flourish.

Tell yourself that you are capable of being discerning in order to see the whole of your life realistically and with personal insight which will propel you forward effectively and satisfactorily.

Now congratulate yourself on your achievements to date and affirm that you can in future carry on the good work which you have undertaken today. And now gently return to full conscious awareness of the present moment.

HIGHER FREQUENCY LAW

Do you truly appreciate that you have everything within you which you might need in order to live a contented and healthy life?

Could you acknowledge and rely on your own intuitive wisdom?

Can you sculpt for yourself a life of peace and tranquillity?

WHAT IS THE NATURAL LAW OF HIGHER FREQUENCY?

The natural law of higher frequency will consider the way in which you embrace spiritual practice and you conduct yourself in your daily life (see Figure 6: *Natural Laws of Higher Frequency*).

The reason why the natural law of higher frequency exists is because you will be equipped with intuitive powers from birth and you can easily realise this potential within yourself throughout your childhood development and your adult maturity.

The natural law of higher frequency will, therefore, assist you to relate to your life and to your existence.

FIGURE 6: NATURAL LAWS OF HIGHER FREQUENCY

VIBRATION	PURIFICATION	PERSPECTIVE	GRATITUDE	GRACE

VIBRATION

The natural law of vibration states that you can become aware of your own feelings, the workings of your physiology and the presence of others.

The law of vibration will, therefore, allow you to develop intuition, sensitivity and psychic abilities. You might, for instance, be able to detect other people's moods and intentions and to appreciate that you know instinctively how to heal yourself.

PURIFICATION

The natural law of purification states that you will be able to undertake self-healing successfully for both your mind and your body as part of your survival mechanism.

The law of purification, therefore, should be your life's goal because you are part of humankind whose duty it is to ensure the continuance of the species. You might, for instance, realise that your mind and body both have a self-healing ability which you can tap into at any time. You might, moreover, find that by seeking alternative therapy and mind healing you can recover from a serious illness provided that you are willing to go the extra mile and to shun unhealthy living and an unproductive lifestyle.

PERSPECTIVE

The natural law of perspective states that you will be able to look at the wider picture in terms of your existence and your interaction with others.

The law of perspective, therefore, will be the balancing agent in your life and within your psyche. You might, for instance, find yourself standing back from a situation or a relationship and then being able to see it more honestly and realistically.

GRATITUDE

The natural law of gratitude states that you will be able to appreciate the benefit of a given circumstance or a lifestyle direction.

The law of gratitude will, therefore, allow you to appreciate the benefits in your life and not to hanker after meaningless material wealth or to be rankled at other people's fortune. You might, for instance, wish to stand back and note the positive things in your life rather than focusing purely on the negative aspects of your existence and what others possess or have achieved.

GRACE

The natural law of grace states that you will be able to attain a state of peace and happiness which will be free of conflict and distress once you have embarked upon your healing journey.

The law of grace will, therefore, allow you to realise that treading a healing path will benefit you in an untold number of ways. You might, for instance, take time out to resolve your dilemmas, to tread the middle ground in life and thereby to find your own personal contentment and concord.

NATURAL LAW OF HIGHER FREQUENCY THERAPEUTIC TEXT

Now may be the time for you to acknowledge your intuitive capacities and to appreciate your instinctual skills.

Sit quietly and merely contemplate your existence.

Many centuries ago when humankind first trod the planet human resources were those things which ensured the survival of both men and women and their offspring. Humankind had to be intuitive and perceptive in order to survive and, therefore, the whole species will be endowed with these attributes which will constitute your inherent survivalist instincts.

All you will need to do now is simply to acknowledge and tap into your intuitive and psychic powers fully.

Acknowledge that as a human being you consist of vibrational energy and that this energy can be harnessed to your advantage.

Celebrate the fact that you are human and can readily utilise your own personal attributes in the social world and when you go about your daily business.

Humankind also possesses a self-healing mechanism which has ensured the continuance of the human species from the very first.

Welcome and rejoice in your self-healing abilities and allow this mechanism to do its work in your best interests. You will, by this means, be able to undertake self-healing and to ensure that the distress of your past experience can be nullified and resolved satisfactorily.

You can assist your self-healing faculty by reflecting on your past experiences and by determining the way in which all your experiences have shaped your current existence. You will then be able to see things in perspective, to view your life realistically and to gain insight from your reflection.

You can also focus on the positive aspects of your existence by way of telling yourself that you do have some factors in your life on which you can count and for which you can be grateful and appreciative.

The more you are able to practice self-healing the more you will be able to attain a state of contentment and grace and be at one with yourself and those about you.

Now let all these thoughts settle so that you can begin to emerge into a new day.

Return into the here-and-now moment only when the time is really right for you.

Now welcome yourself back into a new existence.

SUCCCESS LAW

Can you sometimes feel that you are robbed of your rights in life?

Might you consider that you are undeserving and will never attain your goals?

Do you realise that generosity and consideration of others will reap untold rewards?

WHAT IS THE NATURAL LAW OF SUCCESS?

The natural law of success will consider the extent to which you can safeguard your existence (see Figure 7: *Natural Laws of Success*).

The reason why the natural law of success exists is because you will need to succeed in the social world in some way and to attain those possessions which you will require for a safe and happy existence.

The natural law of success will, therefore, assist you to relate to your fortunes and your misfortunes.

FIGURE 7: NATURAL LAWS OF SUCCESS

| POTENTIAL | GENEROSITY | EFFORT | DESIRE | DETACHMENT | OBLIGATION |

POTENTIAL

The natural law of potential states that you will be able to detect the way in which you can beneficially move forward in life and you can achieve your goals.

The law of potential will, therefore, empower you to see the bigger picture and not hold yourself back unnecessarily. You might, for instance, see the way ahead when in an inclement situation or during a turbulent stage along your life's path.

GENEROSITY

The natural law of generosity states that you can be kind to others as your means of contributing to your social world.

The law of generosity will, therefore, enable you to appreciate yourself unconditionally and to transmit your feelings of wellbeing to others. You might, for instance, feel inclined to acknowledge the support of others and, in turn, to help other individuals accordingly. When you are generous, of course, you will find that others will naturally reciprocate.

Effort

The natural law of effort states that you do not necessarily need to put an inordinate amount of effort into achieving your goals.

The law of effort will, therefore, permit you to unfold aspects of your achievements and the realisation of your goals with a minimal amount of worry and hassle. You might, for instance, be able to satisfy your needs by simply relaxing and allowing life to evolve.

Desire

The natural law of desire states that you will inevitably seek to satisfy your needs as part of your way of attaining happiness and safety.

The law of desire will, therefore, allow you to acknowledge that you have needs and that these requirements can be easily satisfied. You might, for instance, aim to build a better life for yourself by moving house, by changing your job and by not putting up with an unsatisfactory situation.

Detachment

The natural law of detachment states that you will not be able to satisfy your desires by worrying too much about the outcome or the consequences.

The law of detachment will, therefore, enable you to relax and to cease fretting about the future. You might, for instance, notice that if you stop worrying about recovering from an illness then you will naturally heal because you are relaxing and taking care of yourself.

Obligation

The natural law of obligation states that you will have a duty and a responsibility to your family, friends and associates and that honest dealings will pay dividends.

The law of obligation will, therefore, empower you to be considerate of others and not be too acquisitive in your attempt to satisfy your own needs. You might, for instance, reap the rewards of being considerate and acting responsibly towards others which will mean that your personal integrity will remain intact and you will consequently attract worthwhile people into your life.

NATURAL LAW OF SUCCESS THERAPEUTIC TEXT

Perhaps you could envision a rising sun emerging from the horizon?

Can you appreciate the fact that sunrise is an inevitable phenomenon which will happen with certainly every day?

The sun, the moon and the stars do not think about what they are doing because they just do what they have to do every day. Every day the sun rises while the moon is asleep and every night the moon awakes and the stars appear while the sun takes a well-earned rest.

Both the sun and the moon can see that their purpose will be fulfilled every day. The sun and the moon have their place and do their work without any undue effort.

The sun and the moon do not feel that they need to concentrate too hard on their work because their business will occur naturally. The sun and the moon, therefore, can detach from wanting to do their work and simply just get on and do it effectively.

The sun knows what its place is in the sky and can see its potential of bringing light into the cosmos. The moon, conversely, knows its potential as a means of lighting the night sky while allowing the world to sleep, rest and dream.

The sun generously gives its light to the world and brightens your spirits as well as nourishing the flowers and the crops.

The moon casts a shadow which shows the night traveller the way and illuminates the recesses of your mind when you are asleep and dreaming.

Both the sun and the moon have their desires and their goals which they accomplish every day.

The sun will always give light and nourishment to the earth. The moon will always provide illumination and rest and the stars can guide all travellers.

The sun, of course, knows that it will and it must rise in the morning because the planet depends on it even in winter. The moon knows that it must light up the night sky and be the guardian of the world during the night. And both the sun and the moon know and appreciate their obligations and carry out their work relentlessly yet effortlessly and with pleasure.

Saturate your mind with these thoughts so that you can rise and rest at the appropriate times for you and then simply let yourself drift back into the present moment.

Feel enlivened and refreshed from your dream-like experiences when you return to the present moment.

ENERGETIC HEALING

ENERGETIC HEALING

The value of energetic healing will be to empower you to select an appropriate healing route for yourself in order to assist your mind and your body with its self-healing potential.

Energetic healing will help you to appreciate the vibrational composition of your human system.

ENERGETIC HEALING PRACTICE

Do you appreciate that you can go a long way towards helping yourself with a degree of determination?

Can you comprehend that every individual possesses a self-healing mechanism in the interests of the survival of the human species?

Are you aware of your own energetic biosphere and its current state?

WHAT IS ENERGETIC HEALING?

Energetic healing will embrace spiritual healing, meditative practice, psychotherapy and alternative therapy because all these disciplines interact with your body's energetic fields in order to assist your healing journey (see Figure 8: *Energetic Healing*).

FIGURE 8: ENERGETIC HEALING

SPIRITUAL HEALING	MEDITATIVE HEALING	PSYCHOTHERAPY	ALTERNATIVE THERAPY

SPIRITUAL HEALING PRACTICE

Energetic healing can include all forms of spiritual healing, psychic healing or metaphysical healing, such as reiki healing and vortex healing.

Spiritual healing will interact with your energetic biosphere in general and with your physiological and psychological energy systems in particular.

Energy can be channelled into your body and expelled from your body virtually simultaneously guided by your healing practitioner. Your negative energy or stagnant energy, for instance, can be released and then replaced by positive and revitalising healing energy as necessary. As the recipient of energetic healing you yourself will usually dictate whether positive energy will need to be received or negative energy should be discharged or a combination of both.

An energetic healer will normally endeavour to channel positive healing into your system from the top of your head and then help you to expel stale energy out of your body from the soles of your feet. Energetic healing can also be undertaken with imaginative practice or remotely in order to transmit energy over a distance. Energetic healing, consequently, can address both physiological malaise and psychological distress.

Meditative practice

Energetic healing can include self-hypnosis, guided meditation and creative visualisation as well as movement-based practices, such as tai chi and qi gong, which aim to unblock and rebalance your system.

You can undertake meditative practice regularly in order to assist your mind and your body to self-heal and as a means of processing and resolving whatever sits at the top of your healing agenda.

Psychotherapeutic practice

Psychotherapeutic intervention in the form of hypnotherapy, counselling or psychotherapy will assist you specifically with healing psychological wounds as well as related physical malaise.

Psychotherapeutic practice in metaphysical terms will usually comprise hypnotic age-regression and hypnotic past-life regression.

Alternative therapeutic practice

In the arena of alternative therapy and complementary medicine there are many practices which can assist you with your healing journey both from a physiological and a psychological standpoint.

Vibrational medicine, such as homeopathy, vibrational essences and acupuncture, for instance, will endeavour to stimulate your energetic fields directly in order to invoke your inherent self-healing mechanism. Other forms of alternative therapeutic intervention, such as nutritional medicine, herbalism and therapeutic massage, are also an important means by which you can obtain holistic healing.

ENERGETIC FIELDS

Could you ask yourself what you might need to undertake in terms of physiological and psychological healing?

Can you list those areas in your life which could be improved in order to make you healthier, happier and more productive?

Could you congratulate yourself sincerely once you have taken the next important step forward on your healing journey?

WHAT IS AN ENERGETIC FIELD?

The energetic fields (or spiritual bodies) of the human biosphere system will encompass the various electro-magnetic fields (or auric fields) which surround every living creature (see Figure 9: *Energetic Fields*).

Your energetic fields will connect with your viscera, your endocrine system, your nervous system and your energetic channels (or meridian channels).

Your ill-health will be evident as imbalances, blockages or insufficiency in one or more of your energetic fields which energetic healing can address by expelling your unwanted distress and absorbing beneficial vitality.

The energetic fields of your biosphere will consist of the etheric field (or physical body), the mental field (or mental body) and the astral field (or emotional body) of the human system all of which can be used as a channel for energetic healing practice.

FIGURE 9: ENERGETIC FIELDS

FIELD	HUMAN SYSTEM	SYMBOLISM	DENSITY
Etheric	Physical body Anatomy and physiology	Physical malaise	Heavy
Mental	Mental mind Cerebral cortex	Intellectual malaise Conscious mind Rational short-term memory	Medium

Astral	Emotional mind Limbic system	Emotive malaise Unconscious mind Emotive long-term memory	Light

ETHERIC FIELD

The etheric field of the human system will mirror, outline and slightly extend beyond your physical presence and can be seen as the physical auric field by those possessing clairvoyance.

The etheric body will be the densest vibrational energy of the human system because of its connection to your anatomy and physiology.

Your etheric field will require therapeutic assistance if you suffer from any form of ill-health in terms of the functioning of your vital organs and biological systems.

Your etheric field will absorb light and will be the main channel for your vital human life force. The life force is known as chi in Chinese medicine, ki in Japanese terminology, prana in Indian medical practice and great spirit in native American culture.

MENTAL FIELD

The mental field of the human system will embody your conscious mind, your cognitive responses, your communicative ability and your intellect and will constitute your cerebral cortex in physiological terms.

The mental field will be denser than the etheric field but lighter than the astral field because of its association with your intellectual mind.

Your mental field will require therapeutic assistance if you suffer from any type of negative thought patterns, unhelpful beliefs and erroneous assumptions about yourself or others as well as any harmful, unproductive and repetitive motivation.

Your mental body will consist of your concrete thoughts, abstract ideas, logic, short-term memory, rational thinking and general motivational inclinations.

Astral field

The astral field of the human system will consist of your unconscious mind and your emotive responses and will constitute your limbic system in physiological terms.

The astral field will be the lightest vibrational energy of the human system because of its association with your emotive mind. The astral field can be the most complex field because of its intangibility as well as the all-consuming power of your emotive life.

Your astral field will require therapeutic assistance if you suffer from any form of uncontrollable anger, anxiety, guilt or sadness and the negative emotive patterns which these underlying distressful responses will generate.

Your astral field will contain memories of your untoward past experiences, long-held entrenched beliefs and relationship upsets all of which can be regarded as unresolved emotive distress.

Your astral body will also house your long-term memory both from your current life and your past lives according to the doctrine of reincarnation. Your bodily cells will contain imprints from previous generations within your genes which will have been passed down to you through numerous generations and, therefore, can be regarded as memories of past lives. A homeopathic practitioner, for instance, may help you to process your miasms as part of your healing programme. Your miasms will be genetic taints which will have been left over from previous generations when chronic diseases, such as tuberculosis, leprosy and venereal disease, affected the population in epidemic and dramatic proportions.

When healing your astral field all forms of healing can be utilised by your healing practitioner but possibly therapeutic intervention which allows you to investigate your own inner mind at the deepest levels will be the most appropriate.

Meditative healing, creative visualisation and investigative hypnotherapy, therefore, might be your healer's first choice of therapeutic intervention when you seek therapeutic assistance because of the direct access which these practices can afford to your inner mind.

Artistic inspiration, creativity and dream-life will also emanate from your astral field at the centre of your inner mind. Inspiration and creativity from your astral field, combined with mental processes from your mental field, will allow you to make realisations during your healing journey and to bring your creativity and inspiration to the fore.

Access to your astral field will also open up and develop your psychic abilities and thereby your psychic evolution.

ENERGETIC FIELDS THERAPEUTIC TEXT

Maybe you could imagine a golden dawn in which you are evolving?

Notice how slowly and gradually the light enters your existence and how much brighter everything becomes as a result.

A golden dawn will have a healing effect on your body which will enliven your senses and will eradicate your distress in order to further your healing journey.

Focus first on your physical being and notice the way in which you can stimulate healing energy within your energetic fields.

Your auric field will be able to attract light from the golden dawn in order to stimulate and revitalise the principal organs and systems of your physical body.

Your golden dawn will bring with it healing energy in the form of nourishment and sustenance. Your golden dawn will allow toxins to disperse and cells to replenish. Your golden dawn light will reach every crevice and recess of your cellular systems and none will be ignored.

Perhaps you can feel the positive energy entering your body from above and any stagnant energy being simultaneously expelled from the soles of your feet?

Allow this process to continue while you watch it in your mind and remind yourself that the healing process will continue unaided by you as an unstoppable process and without further thought.

Perhaps now you can focus on your mental being?

Can you identify your inner thoughts, ideas, concepts and convictions?

Can you use this special time to weed out negative thoughts and irrational behaviours?

Can you discard unwanted habits and inclinations which are now outmoded and unnecessary?

Can you find a creative way of ceasing to blame yourself for intransigence or inaction?

Can you halt any unhelpful repetitive patterns of behaviour?

Perhaps you can come to the realisation that certain types of behaviour are unproductive and working against your own interests?

Take some time out now to find a means of resolving these dilemmas for yourself and freeing yourself from the chains which bind you to the past.

Now will be the time to consider your feelings and your emotive reactions.

It can now be time to banish those feelings which hold you back from living a free and productive existence.

Look back into the past in order to discover the places where your uncontrollable and unwanted emotive responses were born.

Dredge your unconscious memory and recollections of negative past experiences and decide whether these experiences still need to define you in the future. Make the decision to break the ties of the past which were unhelpful and full of fear, guilt, sadness or anger.

Did you feel afraid when you were bullied at school?

Did you quiver with embarrassment when a teacher told you off in front of your classmates?

Was your family home torn apart when your parents argued violently?

Were you neglected, misunderstood, ill-considered or abused as a child?

Did one or more of your beloved parents die early in your life?

Were you ill-treated by an ex-partner or a spouse?

Was life not the way you would have wished it to be in the past?

Take action in order to allow your inner mind to resolve your outstanding dilemmas with certainty of success.

Can you visualise a scenario in which you can find a creative means of solving your dilemmas now about your thoughts, your feelings and your motivation?

Can you find a way of putting the record straight in your mind?

What would you like to change about the past in your imagination?

Can you speak to someone from your past and tell it like it is?

Can you explain to yourself that during childhood you were vulnerable and naive?

Can you see yourself as a little child who was not worldly-wise and so believed everything which others told him/her?

Are you aware that when you were a child your so-called elders and betters were not actually those super gods whom you trusted implicitly?

Now let all your thoughts and feelings settle into that place which allows the deepest healing to take place. Feel the power of your self-healing attributes and know that you are the sole agency for moving forward towards another golden dawn.

And when you are sure – really sure – that you have completed your valuable work for today then spend some time congratulating yourself on what you have achieved and what you can take forward with you for the future before returning to the here-and-now moment.

Simply open your eyes gently when the time is right for you.

Chakra Healing

CHAKRA HEALING

The value of chakra healing will be to enable to you seek an appropriate form of mind-body healing for yourself.

Chakra healing will focus on both your physical and your emotional malaise in the healing context.

CHAKRA HEALING PRACTICE

Can you decide which aspects of your physiological and psychological distress are at the top of your personal agenda for healing?

Could you make a list of those therapeutic interventions which you would consider are most appropriate for your healing needs?

Can you imagine your bodily systems and your mind's faculties in conjunction in order to appreciate your total healing picture?

What is chakra healing?

The chakra healing system will consist of seven dense-energy lower chakras and five light-energy higher chakras which collectively will comprise the twelve-chakra system (see Figure 10: *Twelve-Chakra System*).

The twelve-chakra system will be a ripe medium for energetic healing through both the lower chakra system which will relate to your body and the higher chakra system which will relate to your mind.

Your etheric field will house your lower chakra system which in western physiological parlance will be the equivalent of your endocrine system.

Your mental field and your astral field will house your higher chakra system which in western physiological parlance will be the equivalent of your cerebral cortex and your limbic system.

Each chakra within the twelve-chakra system will embody an energetic vortex which will be in balance in health or out of balance in ill-health.

When undertaking any form of psycho-spiritual healing you and your practitioner will be working directly or indirectly with your total twelve-chakra system in order to release stagnant energy and to replace this negativity with beneficial energy which will generate better physiological and psychological health.

The chakra system is a concept taken originally from oriental philosophy but which will directly relate to western medical knowledge in the case of the lower chakra system and metaphysical law in the case of the higher chakra system. The chakra healing process, therefore, will propel you along your mind-body curative path and will allow you to evolve spiritually.

FIGURE 10: TWELVE-CHAKRA SYSTEM

LOWER CHAKRA SYSTEM	HIGHER CHAKRA SYSTEM
Seven physiological chakras Etheric field Endocrine system	Five psychological chakras Mental & astral fields Cerebral cortex & limbic system

LOWER CHAKRA SYSTEM

Could you imagine your energetic fields and note the colours which your auric field contains?

Can you scan your auric field in order to discover what comes to mind about your health and wellbeing?

Could you use your meditative practice in order to guide you towards taking the next step on your healing journey?

WHAT IS THE LOWER CHAKRA SYSTEM?

The lower chakra system will relate to the human body in terms of your anatomy and physiology (see Figure 11: *Lower Chakra System*).

Your seven lower energetic chakras will consist of the dense energetic matter associated with your physicality. Although this is not an exact science each lower chakra will approximately correspond with one of the endocrine glands. Your endocrine system (or hormonal system) will be responsible for regulating your health by the secretion of hormonal substances (or biochemical messengers). Each endocrine gland will produce a hormone which will help to regulate the major organs and principal systems of your body in order to maintain your full functionality and wellbeing.

Each lower chakra will be associated with an archetypal focus in the healing context which will be addressed when you receive healing in order to boost the positive energy around the chakra in question.

Each chakra has been named according to its location in your body and has a vibrational colour which can be seen by those with developed clairvoyant faculties.

FIGURE 11: LOWER CHAKRA SYSTEM

NUMBER	NAME	COLOUR	HUMAN SYSTEM	SYMBOLISM
1	Root	Red	Eliminative system	Self-empowerment
2	Sacral	Orange	Reproductive system	Self-nurturing

3	Solar plexus	Yellow	Digestive system	Courage
4	Heart	Pink	Circulatory system	Self-regard
4	Heart	Green	Immune system	Generosity
5	Throat	Blue	Metabolic system	Communication
6	Brow	Purple	Endocrine system	Intuition
7	Crown	White	Nervous system	Self-knowledge

ROOT CHAKRA

The root chakra (or base chakra) will be located at the base of your spine as the lower extremity of your nervous system.

The root chakra will be associated with your eliminative organs which will serve as a means of expelling toxins and waste products from your system.

Energetically your root chakra will be linked to self-empowerment and your zest for survival.

Your root chakra in the healing context, therefore, will help you to relinquish intransigence which will hold you back from achieving your potential and will propel you forward with a positive driving force in order to attain your goals.

The root chakra can be seen energetically as red in colour at a vibrational level.

SACRAL CHAKRA

The sacral chakra will be located in your genital region and pelvic area.

The sacral chakra will be associated with your reproductive organs which will define your gender and will allow you to reproduce and pass on your genetic inherence to your progeny.

Energetically your sacral chakra will be linked to your self-nurturing, the care of your offspring and your perception of your own sexuality.

Your sacral chakra in the healing context, therefore, will help you to release any negative self-image and self-sacrificial tendencies which you may retain and will enhance your ability to procreate and to nurture healthy intimate relationships.

The sacral chakra can be seen energetically as orange in colour at a vibrational level.

SOLAR PLEXUS

The solar plexus chakra will be located around the complex of digestive organs which will consist of your stomach, liver, gall bladder, pancreas, intestines and digestive tract.

The solar plexus chakra will be associated with your ability to intake and digest nourishment in order to maintain your health and to prolong your existence. Your digestive tract, moreover, will embody your enteric nervous system which will generate your gut-reaction to people and to situations in the external world.

Energetically your solar plexus chakra will be linked to your ability to face life in all its many raw, unpredictable and diverse facets.

Your solar plexus in the healing context, therefore, will help you to consider the extent of your courage and self-confidence as you face the external world and your ability to handle social experience.

The solar plexus chakra can be seen energetically as yellow in colour at a vibrational level.

HEART CHAKRA

The heart chakra will be located around your heart and thymus gland region within your chest and will be associated with both your circulatory system and your immune system both of which will reach every component of your physical being.

The heart chakra will be associated with the circulation of your blood because your heart is a life-maintaining pump. Your heart chakra, moreover, will relate to your thymus gland which will regulate your immune system as your interface with the outside world.

Energetically your heart chakra will govern the way in which you love yourself and your consequent love and regard of others. When you are understanding and appreciative of yourself you will naturally banish any self-hatred and will be accepting and generous towards your fellow creatures.

Your heart chakra in the healing context, therefore, will help you to promote self-love rather than self-blame which will have a positive knock-on effect for you in terms of your interaction with society.

The heart chakra can be seen energetically as both pink and green in colour at a vibrational level.

THROAT CHAKRA

The throat chakra will be located around your throat and neck area which will house your vocal apparatus.

The throat chakra will be associated with your voice and your communication with others. Your throat chakra will be situated in the region of your thyroid gland which will govern your metabolism as your means of maintaining the optimal functioning of all your bodily cells and systems.

Energetically your throat chakra will dictate your general health and your energy resources as well as your ability to speak up for yourself, to tell it like it is and to communicate effectively with those around you.

Your throat chakra in the healing context, therefore, will help you to find your voice, to state your opinions honestly, to be truthful with yourself and not to allow others to control you or to overwhelm you.

The throat chakra can be seen energetically as blue in colour at a vibrational level.

BROW CHAKRA

The brow chakra will be located at your forehead, face and eyes.

The brow chakra will be associated with the core of your endocrine system which will be responsible for regulating all your body's hormonal activity. Your pituitary gland (or hypophysis) will be the orchestrator of your endocrine system and will be closely linked to your nervous system.

The brow chakra, moreover, will house your pineal gland (or epiphysis cerebri) as the source of your vision because this gland will regulate your waking-hours and your sleeping-patterns which will be governed by daylight. Your brow chakra and your pineal gland, moreover, will govern your clairvoyant faculties as the third eye (or anya).

Your brow chakra in the healing context, therefore, will enhance your perception of the world about you and will fine-tune your intuition while simultaneously releasing negative misconceptions which you may hold about yourself and others whom you encounter.

The brow chakra can be seen energetically as purple in colour at a vibrational level.

CROWN CHAKRA

The crown chakra will be located at the top of your head and will surround your brain as the upper extremity of your nervous system.

The crown chakra will be associated with the functioning of your central nervous system in particular and your peripheral nervous system by implication. The crown chakra will, moreover, be your link between living in this world and your contact with the spiritual realm.

Your crown chakra in the healing context, therefore, will allow you to receive life-affirming energy which can assist you to achieve overall wellbeing and can enhance your self-knowledge as the gateway to the higher energetic chakras.

The crown chakra can be seen energetically as white in colour at a vibrational level.

LOWER CHAKRA SYSTEM THERAPEUTIC TEXT

Allow yourself to relax deeply in a sense which you might not have thought at all possible before.

Help yourself to imagine a beautiful rainbow which surrounds you and yet is contained within you. A rainbow appears when the sun and the rain are in perfect conjunction.

Now imagine that you are passing through the red of your healing rainbow and that the colour red is embracing you and surrounding you.

Red is the colour of fire, energy and life.

Red is the power within you which you may have so far not recognised within yourself.

Simply unleash that bright power now and claim it as your own. Feel that red colour permeating your soul and unleashing your primal power to live, to thrive and to flourish. If you find that you cannot reach your own powerhouse of energy then simply pause here while your mind finds a way of rectifying this situation.

Now imagine yourself being enfolded by the orange in your healing rainbow.

Orange is the colour of sand, blazing skies and fruitfulness.

Allow the orange to float into your being and consume you with self-nurturing. The orange represents the core of your being and defines you as a member of humankind. You may be a parent who has raised children, cared for them lovingly and nurtured them through their formative years. You may feel inclined to recall your own upbringing which, if it was less than somewhat, could have left a painful scar.

Now will be the time to heal that wound by embracing the orange within your healing rainbow and letting that orange heal the scars of your manhood/womanhood so that you can unite with yourself and with others.

Once you have allowed the orange to settle peacefully within you perhaps you could now turn to the yellow in your healing rainbow?

Yellow is the colour of sunshine and bright summer days when the river is in full spate and flowers are in full bloom.

Yellow represents your courage and your ability to face your fears and tears and even to embrace the healing process which initially may seem daunting. You can easily overcome any troubles which you may have by facing them head on and then embracing your healing mission with open arms.

The feeling of welcoming in the yellow within your healing rainbow will unlock doors of light for you which you might hitherto not have realised you could open. Just enable the process to occur without putting any effort into your healing voyage and allow time for this process to naturally evolve.

Now turn your attention to the green within your healing rainbow.

Green is the colour of health, nature and plenty.

The green in your healing rainbow will be the very depths of your soul healing where self-nurturing and self-love become part of your whole existence and daily life. Summon all the powers within you which can invoke this form of healing by allowing the green of your healing rainbow to flood your auric field and wait until this process is complete before moving to the next stage.

Once the green of your healing rainbow has entered your auric field so that you can love yourself totally then invite in the pink in your healing rainbow.

Pink is the colour of love, flowers and gaiety.

When you love yourself then you can easily feel love and compassion for others and indeed for the whole of humanity.

When you embrace the pink in your healing rainbow you will naturally begin to appreciate that others need to be blamed for the wrongs which they might have done to you in the past but, in the process, you will come to accept all humanity and consign your justifiable feelings of anger and resentment to insignificance.

If you do not blame others appropriately then the likelihood is that you will blame yourself and so retain your pain and self-loathing. If you apportion blame appropriately then you can let your hurt feelings diminish and you will not blame those people in your current life who are, in essence, trustworthy.

Give yourself sufficient time to enable this process to occur naturally before moving to the next stage of your therapeutic journey through the healing rainbow.

Let yourself now explore the blue in your healing rainbow.

Blue is the colour of communication and freedom of speech.

Permit yourself to tell it like it is and speak the truth to yourself and others. The blue in your healing rainbow will represent your inner voice which will be the key to your personal truth.

Allow the blue in your healing rainbow to envelop you in a way which you might not have thought possible before. Allow the blue in your healing rainbow to rest and relax you still further.

See yourself speaking up for yourself, telling it like it is and confronting those who were in truth your wrongdoers. Do not hide your voice under a bushel but set it free in the air. Imagine this process of finding your own true voice and speaking up for yourself. Permit this important part of your voyage to occur naturally and effortlessly.

Now you can turn to the purple in your healing rainbow because purple represents your intuition and your personal insight which will now be beginning to emerge naturally and burgeon from deep within your soul.

Purple is the colour of your intuition and your psychic abilities.

When you start to excavate your inner self, to speak up for yourself and to learn to love yourself more then you will find your intuition beginning to grow and blossom effortlessly.

The more you look inwardly at yourself the more you will discover that your intuition and insight are strong and flourishing.

This will be the moment at which you will start to get to know yourself as you have never done before and it could change your life for the better forever. Relax still further and just allow this process to occur naturally without any conscious thought.

Perhaps it is time now to explore the white in your healing rainbow?

White is the colour of purity, peace and a blank canvas.

The white in your healing rainbow will depict your higher self and that part of you in which all your past healing comes together. The white part of your being knows everything there is to know about you and will unlock the door to your personal wisdom and purity of thought. Allow this part of you to settle as the fulfilment of this aspect of your healing journey.

You may from now on rest assured that the white in your healing rainbow will continue to show you more and more about yourself so that you can achieve infinite peace and self-knowledge.

Perhaps you can now congratulate yourself on what you have achieved here today by passing through your healing rainbow?

And pause to see if there is any part of your healing rainbow to which you would like to return for a second look.

Give yourself plenty of time now to return to those areas which might need further and special attention and take a moment to allow your mind to settle and resolve whatever needs to be addressed in the here-and-now.

And when you are really sure that you have done everything which you possibly can for yourself today and have thoroughly congratulated yourself on your remarkable achievements now simply allow yourself to return slowly and gently to full waking consciousness.

HIGHER CHAKRA SYSTEM

Can you ask your inner mind to tell you what you perceive about yourself and your therapeutic journey?

Could you scan your life in order to highlight those times when you have suffered from distress?

Can you ask yourself what your inner mind is telling you about your emotions and your feelings?

WHAT IS THE HIGHER CHAKRA SYSTEM?

The higher chakra system will encompass five energetic chakras above your crown chakra which can receive healing energy (see Figure 12: *Higher Chakra System*).

These higher spiritual chakras will be the energy centres of your higher awareness and will be the product of your mind's experience and emotive perception which will be contained within your total biosphere.

Emotive and psychological healing can take place with both current-life age-regression and past-life regression in order to access your inner mind. Exploration of your higher chakra system will, therefore, constitute the true core of your healing journey.

FIGURE 12: HIGHER CHAKRA SYSTEM

NUMBER	NAME	COLOUR	SYMBOLISM
8	Higher self	Silver	Unconscious mind Self-awareness
9	Soul wisdom	Gold	Personal life path Personal truth
10	Synchronicity	Platinum	Personal evolution Self-empowerment

11	Soul journey	Clear	Intuitive development Psychic ability
12	Cosmic connection	Black	Personal peace Authenticity

HIGHER SELF CHAKRA

The higher self chakra will consist of the totality of your unconscious mind and will initiate your healing journey in both your current life and your past lives.

Your higher self will evolve during your healing journey and the more therapeutic intervention which you undertake the more you will become aware of yourself and the world about you. The therapeutic healing process will stimulate you in order to excavate negativity and to resolve unpleasant distress from your unconscious mind.

Your newfound self-discovery now can become part of your experience because you are more self-aware and less prone to uncontrollable emotive reactions and self-destructive tendencies. The process of self-healing will provide you with an untold degree of freedom, will impact on your motivation and will influence all your relationships and interaction with others.

The higher self chakra can be seen energetically as silver in colour at a vibrational level.

SOUL WISDOM CHAKRA

The soul wisdom chakra will reveal your exemplary qualities, inherent talents, intrinsic personality traits and your ability to make the appropriate choices for yourself as you journey through your life.

Your soul wisdom chakra will permit you to fulfil your soul contract as that pattern which has been set out for you at birth. You might, for instance, be destined to be an artist, a teacher or a healer and this knowledge will reveal itself as you begin to tread the appropriate path in order to realise your true potential.

The soul wisdom chakra can be seen energetically as gold in colour at a vibrational level.

Synchronicity chakra

The synchronicity chakra will bring together all your skills, talents, self-knowledge, self-awareness and healthy self-perceptions in order to allow you to become the person you were really intended to be.

Your synchronicity chakra will allow you to benefit from the wisdom which you have gained from your healing journey and the means by which you can attain contentment in life.

The synchronicity chakra can be seen energetically as platinum in colour at a vibrational level.

Soul journey chakra

The soul journey chakra will be concerned with your intuitive ability as well as your clairvoyance, clairaudience and clairsentience.

Your soul journey chakra will empower you to become more intuitive and psychic because of your healing journey and the self-awareness which you will have acquired in the process. Knowledge of yourself will hence allow you to understand and be more compassionate towards others whom previously you might have judged unfavourably.

The soul journey chakra can be seen energetically as clear in colour at a vibrational level.

Cosmic connection chakra

The cosmic connection chakra will be the culmination of all the learning which you have acquired on your therapeutic healing voyage from which you can fully reap the benefits.

Your cosmic connection chakra will relieve you of physiological and psychological ill-health, negative reactions, unhelpful thoughts, unwanted habits, unproductive motivation and dysfunctional relationships. From this vantage point you can now be understanding and considerate of yourself and your fellow-travellers. At this stage you will have discovered your true self and your true path in life which will lead to personal contentment and fruitfulness.

The cosmic connection chakra can be seen energetically as black in colour at a vibrational level.

HIGHER CHAKRA SYSTEM THERAPEUTIC TEXT

Be aware that you are a constantly evolving being from the moment of your conception onwards to the present and indeed into the future.

Contemplate this notion and allow yourself to drift into your own mind in order to access that place where only you can go.

Empower yourself to relax with this thought in mind.

Welcome yourself heartily to your journey of healing exploration from this special place in your mind.

Consider that when you open your own mind you will reach a new world with a spirit of wonderment and amazement.

Can you find the key to your own soul by considering yourself as a unique individual?

Can you appreciate that your reaction to all your life's experiences will be unique to you?

Could you acknowledge that you can easily access your thoughts about yourself and so make many interesting self-discoveries?

You will be able to become more self-aware with every moment once you have looked carefully and honestly into your unique mind wherein sits all the knowledge which will be available to you.

Can you consider the person you are as a unique individual?

Are you aware of your personal strengths and talents?

Can you appreciate your personal gifts and inclinations?

Are you satisfied with the path which you are treading in life or would you like your existence to change radically?

Can you find the key to opening up the box which will allow you to be yourself without any apology?

Now look at the way in which you regard yourself.

Do you believe that you are undeserving or that you are inferior to others perhaps?

Are you inclined to deny yourself pleasures?

Do you worry far too much about what other people might be thinking about you?

Are you unnecessarily putting yourself down when you should be promoting your happiness and branching out into new territories?

Have you considered your intuitive abilities and your psychic powers as part of your growing self-awareness and self-acceptance?

Can you find a foolproof means of healing those aspects of your existence which are holding you back from becoming truly fulfilled?

Are you able to find a magic way of fulfilling your potential in life by expanding your thinking and your outlook?

Would you like to give yourself permission to relinquish the anguish of the past which might inhibit you?

Would you care to set yourself free from those emotive reactions which are unprofitable?

Are you willing to break those unproductive habits which do not serve your best interests?

All these goals can be naturally achieved by accessing your higher chakra system which holds the key to all your life history, your future potential and your full self-awareness.

Invite yourself, therefore, to take the next step of your healing journey and relish the prospect of what it might hold for you personally.

Settle now into the knowledge that things will be different in the future.

Start now to awaken yourself to an exciting prospect of what is to come.

Simply return to the present moment refreshed and knowledgeable when you feel ready and able to move forward. And consider the ways in which you have benefited from your experience today.

AGE-REGRESSION

Have you ever considered the effect of your childhood distress on your current life?

Can you invite yourself to view the past with the benefit of hindsight?

Do you realise that everything which has occurred in your life will have had an inevitable effect on you?

WHAT IS AGE-REGRESSION?

Age regression will be an imaginative means of accessing your inner mind in the therapeutic context and, thereby, can assist you to heal your higher chakra system.

Age-regression will enable you to relinquish distressing emotive reactions which have accumulated as a direct result of your past experiences and have left an unwelcomed legacy with you.

Age regression will facilitate the exploration of your past stressful-traumatic experience throughout your life. Your current-day distress will normally have its roots in childhood and in your formative years. If you have experienced any overwhelming tragedy in your adult life you will almost certainly need additionally to deal with the backlog of your childhood distress.

AGE-REGRESSION THERAPEUTIC TEXT

Relax into yourself and permit yourself to enter a phase of contemplation.

Let your inner mind step off the roundabout of life and put aside those tasks and thoughts which would normally demand your attention.

Settle your inner mind into a deeply relaxed state and cast aside the cares of the day.

Focus on the depths of your inner mind in order to visualise where you are currently and where you would like to be in the future in terms of your healing journey.

Now take yourself down deeper into your state of relaxation so that you can peer into your inner mind in a very special way and review your life.

Consider what your life's journey has been so far, where you have travelled, who you have met and what adventures you have encountered along the way.

See yourself moving through your adult life and examining every aspect of your current existence. Look at your work, your family, your status and your play activities in this world as your habitat.

Look at your current family life with a partner and children.

Maybe also consider the occupation which you have chosen for yourself?

Think about where you are living and whether the place is right for you.

Ask yourself honestly whether you regard your current life as satisfactory and then answer your own probing questions realistically because you cannot actually deceive yourself.

Are you truly happy and contented with life or dissatisfied and frustrated?

Do you feel fulfilled or discontent?

Do you feel empty and lonely?

Do you consider that you have made a success of life and are you sincerely happy with your achievements?

Is there any area of your current life which displeases you?

Review your life by going back to the time when you were at school and had not yet experienced the wide world and independent life as an adult.

Look at what life was like when you first went to school as a young child and how you might have been daunted by the prospect of leaving home for the first time.

Were the other children at school happy and playful or were they unkind and bullying?

As you progressed through the school system did you enjoy your studies or did you feel that the whole experience was boring and hostile?

Now review that time before you ever even went to school when you were at home with Mum and your siblings or simply alone on your own.

Can you explore those aspects of your childhood with perhaps long-forgotten memories which are still near at hand in your mind?

Recall your family life as a child with your parents or guardians and your siblings if you had any. Bring to mind how life was back then at home, at play and at school.

What was your family life like?

Was your childhood a delightful and enjoyable experience?

Were you happy and full of life?

Was your childhood somehow untoward?

Did Mum and Dad work too hard and so you never saw them much?

Did Mum and Dad row a lot?

Was one of your parents not there for you because he/she was physically or emotionally absent?

Most important of all – did you feel loved and appreciated?

Were you neglected or unloved at any time in your childhood or later on?

Did you feel misunderstood, hated, ill-used or abused during your early years?

Again be truly honest with yourself in order to unearth those most unpleasant experiences in your early life so that you can consider the effect which these events have had on you.

When you are troubled in early life then the impact of this distress will generate a lasting legacy which will stay with you throughout your entire life until the tide begins to turn.

Ensure that you can tell it like it is and cry any uncried tears, shake out any stultifying fears, relieve yourself of any crippling guilt and express your justifiable anger at anything and everything unpleasant and unfair which has occurred to you in the past.

Apportion blame appropriately at the door of those people who have wronged you or those situations which have worked against you. Do not blame yourself for those things which are the responsibility of others. It is not profitable to protect others who have ill-treated you in the past.

So further your healing journey by sorting these things out honestly and truthfully. But give yourself time for these notions to settle.

When you feel that you have covered a great deal of ground by facing up to your personal truth then relax into the feeling that you have done good work for the day.

Now just very slowly and gently bring yourself back into the present moment in order to continue with the business of the day happy in the knowledge that you have achieved much for yourself today.

PAST-LIFE REGRESSION

Might you concede that your cellular memory will contain imprints from your genetic history?

Can you imagine a different life which actually resembles your current existence?

Could you accept that an investigation into symbolic imagery about an entire alien existence could empower you spiritually?

WHAT IS PAST-LIFE REGRESSION?

Past-life regression will be an imaginative means of accessing your genetic memory in the therapeutic context and, thereby, can assist you to heal your higher chakra system.

Past-life regression will facilitate the exploration of your past genetic history which is energetically contained within your cellular DNA.

You can regard past-life regression as a literal means of revisiting a previous existence in a relaxed state of mind in accordance with metaphysical doctrine. You can, alternatively, merely consider the therapeutic methodology of past-life regression as having a symbolic value for you in terms of looking at your current life and your distress from a different angle which can mitigate the pain of your ongoing experiences today.

PAST-LIFE REGRESSION THERAPEUTIC TEXT

> *Can you imagine yourself floating on a cloud which can carry you through the mists of time in peace and tranquillity?*
>
> *Allow this sensation to reach your inner mind so that you can focus on ridding yourself of unpleasant and distressing pain and suffering.*
>
> *Perhaps you can imagine yourself in the womb long before you ever set foot on the planet?*
>
> *Few people can actually remember what it was like to be in the womb but you will be able to imagine this experience.*
>
> *Can you visualise who was there at your birth and what they were thinking and feeling at the time?*

Can you feel the atmosphere which surrounded your time in the womb and during your birth?

Let yourself explore what life was like before you were ever conceived.

Perhaps you can imagine some previous existence in which you were somehow different from the way you are now?

This will be a journey for you simply in your imaginative mind which you can enjoy and explore to your heart's content.

Could you imagine yourself in another time, another place and another existence?

Can you imagine being born into a different age?

Perhaps your mind will take you to the last century or even the one before?

Can you see yourself as living in the Stone Age or in the Bronze Age?

Can you behold yourself as a warrior or a king?

Might you imagine being a pauper or a lord of the manor?

Could you be living in a far-off land of primitive people or those with many riches?

Might your mind be showing you ancient Greece or Rome?

You may not know where your mind will take you on its flight of fancy but your mind will know exactly what you might need to revisit from any former life or lives.

So just relax still further and allow your mind to do its work. In a moment you can ask yourself where you find yourself so that you can explore what your mind is now showing you.

And when you are ready just simply convey your thoughts to yourself but still remain very relaxed.

Take your time in viewing your thoughts and fully experience what might be happening to you. Note what you are thinking and feeling. Notice what you can see and who is around you.

Are you in a friendly or a hostile environment?

Are you facing danger?

Are you confused by events and those around you?

Note every detail of what you are experiencing.

See where you find yourself and invite yourself to explore this territory in depth in order to further your healing journey.

If you are in distress can you find a creative way of resolving this situation for yourself by perhaps inviting a helper into the picture?

Can you grow in stature until you are big enough and strong enough to face your foes and to conquer the situation?

Could you fight the tiger or defend those whom you might seek to protect using your own strength?

Might you be able to get yourself out of a terrifying situation as if by the magic power of your own imagination?

Once you have resolved your distress perhaps you can sit back and evaluate your experience?

Can you note the power and strength within you which has enabled you to overcome a disaster?

Now will be the time to allow your healing to settle and for you to relax back into the peace and tranquillity of your current existence by bringing yourself gently back into the here-and-how moment at this time.

But only return to the present moment when your work for the day is truly completed and your journey has reached its destination.

Take your time to bring yourself back through the ages or the places which you have visited where you have discovered much about yourself.

Welcome back to this world with your new-found knowledge and wisdom knowing that you can return to that other place at any time in the future when you need to explore those aspects of your former existence in more detail if necessary.

ANGELIC HEALING

ANGELIC HEALING

The value of angelic healing will be to enable you to make contact with vibrational beings outside your normal realm of existence and experience.

Angelic healing will permit you to imaginatively reach cosmic light beings who are able to assist you with your healing journey.

ANGELIC HEALING PRACTICE

Could you appreciate the symbolic value of visualising angelic guidance?

Can you imagine that you are supported by an imaginary friend?

Do you see yourself in isolation from the rest of the universe?

What is angelic healing?

The angelic healing hierarchy will comprise your personal guardian angels and archangels together with the ascended masters and the lords of karma (see Figure 13: *Angelic Healing*).

With angelic healing you can summon the assistance of the angelic hierarchy when receiving healing yourself or when providing healing for another. These light beings will exist to help you as an incarnated being in order to progress along your spiritual path.

Your guardian angels (or angelic spirit guides) will help you on a daily basis while the archangels will assist you when summoned. These angels will be supported by the ascended masters who will bring spiritual wisdom to the cosmos and the lords of karma who will keep the akashic records (or karmic records) of your soul's evolution through several lifetimes.

When working with the angelic realm you should be aware that your progress will occur naturally with therapeutic intervention and that you will not need to force yourself unnaturally to adopt a given lifestyle or a specific mindset.

Your therapeutic journey with angelic healing will allow you to resolve the root cause of your dilemmas in order to unravel the impact which your past history has exacted according to the cause-and-effect principle.

The benefit of unwinding of your dilemmas from the past will be to enhance your self-image, to strengthen your self-concept and to improve your relationships with others. Your therapeutic progress will also enable you to relieve yourself of unwanted habits, to relinquish your uncontrollable emotive reactions, to make your own choices in life and to become fulfilled.

If you find the concept of angelic healing difficult to accept then simply appreciate and utilise the symbolic significance of working with these healing concepts without taxing your belief system too severely.

FIGURE 13: ANGELIC HEALING

GUARDIAN ANGELS	ARCHANGELS	ASCENDED MASTERS	LORDS OF KARMA

GUARDIAN ANGELS

Do you believe that you are alone in the world?

Can you appreciate that you can call for spiritual help when required?

Might you feel that help is near at hand and within your auric field?

What is a guardian angel?

Your guardian angels will be one or more personal angels who have been assigned to you in order to assist you with your healing journey throughout your life.

Your guardian angels will reside close within your auric field in order to provide you with instant assistance when you might require help.

Guardian angels will, moreover, play a special role when you are rendering healing assistance to another because these spirit guides can summon additional help as required from the whole of the healing hierarchy.

You can even regard your personal angels as an extension of your inner mind. You could, therefore, consider your guardian angels to be a way of merely communicating with yourself rather than being an entity outside yourself.

Guardian angels therapeutic text

Settle yourself smoothly in a relaxed place and at a time when you will not be disturbed. Sink into your inner mind and enjoy the luxury of tranquillity and peace.

Calm your mind softly and gently and let go of the troubles of the day. Take time out of your busy life for yourself now.

Could you maybe imagine yourself floating in a mist and following a trail of fairy dust?

Allow the mist to lead you forward as if by magic. See yourself moving along a mysterious path which is designed for you to discover more about yourself.

Perhaps your path will guide you upwards or along a winding trail?

Maybe your path will move you forward rapidly or leisurely?

Could your route be taking you up a mountain or into the woods?

Might your path be reaching the stars or exploring the clouds?

Just permit yourself to define your own journey and where it will lead you.

Perhaps you will see a mountain in the distance which rises up to meet the skyline?

Maybe you will see a castle looming large before your eyes?

Or possibly you will encounter a clearing in the forest which holds a special magic for you?

Now perhaps the mist can clear and you can look around the place which you have discovered for yourself?

Is there a wise oracle at the top of your mountain?

Is there a welcoming door into your castle?

Could you find a hut in the forest clearing?

Or maybe you can simply see a place to which you are drawn because your guardian angels are leading you there?

Can you discover your guardian angels in your chosen place and become acquainted now with these beings of light?

Allow yourself to be embraced and welcomed. Receive the power and guidance which you might need from your guardian angels who may have a special message for you right now. Familiarise yourself with the way in which you can work with your personal angels in order to heal yourself and perhaps others.

Record this experience in your mind as a landmark along the journey which your soul is taking. Even when you retrace your steps back along your misty path you will seem to retain the imprint of this important experience of meeting with your personal angelic spirit guides.

Allow your mind, body and soul to absorb your special experience and your meeting with these angelic beings and let the encounter change your life forever.

And when you really feel that the time is right for you to move forward with this additional aid then just stir yourself slowly and gently in order to continue with the business of the day but with a new spring in your step.

ARCHANGELS

Do you feel that there is a higher power out there just waiting to assist you on your healing journey?

Might you believe that you could heal yourself with some angelic help?

Can you feel a connection with the rest of the cosmos?

WHAT IS AN ARCHANGEL?

The archangels will be concerned with the bigger picture of humanity and each archangel will have a special healing mission for the cosmos of which you are important part (see Figure 14: *Archangels*).

Your personal healing programme will be supervised by one or more of the archangels who will initiate healing through your twelve-chakra system.

FIGURE 14: ARCHANGELS

ARCHANGEL	SYMBOLISM
Uriel	Intuition
Gabriel	Communication
Jophiel	Art
Raphael	Healing
Chamuel	Self-love
Michael	Protection
Raziel	Inspiration
Zadkiel	Compassion
Haniel	Self-fulfilment
Metatron	Healing

URIEL

Archangel Uriel will oversee the development of your intuitive and self-awareness powers in order to ensure your survival in the social world. Archangel Uriel will, therefore, assist you to become more attuned to yourself and will help you to gain awareness of those with whom you come into contact.

GABRIEL

Archangel Gabriel will oversee the development of your social communication and your academic study which will bring you enlightenment. Archangel Gabriel will, therefore, allow you to broaden your knowledge of the world and your existence.

JOPHIEL

Archangel Jophiel will oversee the development of your creative talents. Archangel Jophiel will, therefore, nurture your creativity, your artistic ability and your appreciation of aesthetic beauty.

RAPHAEL

Archangel Raphael will oversee the development of your mind, body and spirit. Archangel Raphael will, therefore, enable you to attain your inner harmony and to maintain your personal health.

CHAMUEL

Archangel Chamuel will oversee the development of your peaceful and harmonious relationships with yourself and with others. Archangel Chamuel will, therefore, promote your ability to interact successfully in the social world.

MICHAEL

Archangel Michael will oversee the development of your personal protection and your ability to defend yourself in times of crises. Archangel Michael will, therefore, help you to ensure your survival as a member of humankind.

Raziel

Archangel Raziel will oversee the development of your personal insight and physic gifts. Archangel Raziel will, therefore, encourage you to develop your spiritual insight and your psychic perception.

Zadkiel

Archangel Zadkiel will oversee the development of your compassion and empathy towards yourself and others. Archangel Zadkiel will, therefore, facilitate the development of your ability to love yourself and those who are important in your life.

Haniel

Archangel Haniel will oversee the development of your happiness and contentment. Archangel Haniel will, therefore, allow you to attain self-fulfilment in life by pursing your life's mission and realising your aspirations.

Metatron

Archangel Metatron will oversee the development of the way in which you choose to assist others with their pain and suffering as a result of your own healing voyage. Archangel Metatron will, therefore, enable you to be of service to others as an integral part of your own healing journey.

Energetic healing links to angelic healing

There are links between your chakra systems and the archangels who will assist you with your healing mission (see Figure 15: *Energetic Healing Links to Angelic Healing*).

Consider the implications of the work of your personal archangels and the way in which these light beings can assist you with your healing journey through your twelve-chakra system.

Figure 15: Energetic Healing Links to Angelic Healing

Archangel	Chakra
Uriel	Root

Gabriel	Sacral
Jophiel	Solar plexus
Raphael	Heart
Chamuel	Heart
Michael	Throat
Raziel	Brow
Zadkiel	Crown
Haniel	Higher self
Metatron	Soul wisdom

ARCHANGELS THERAPEUTIC TEXT

Make yourself comfortable and relax deeply in a way which removes you from the everyday world of work and business.

Allow this feeling of sinking into yourself to grow gradually.

Invite archangel Uriel to visit you in order to reflect on your intuitive powers which will help you to understand others as well as yourself.

Archangel Uriel can serve you by making you more aware of your own inner wisdom and your personal truth. Allow this knowledge to seep into your soul.

Perhaps you may wish to consult archangel Gabriel who will help you when you interact and communicate with others?

Archangel Gabriel will assist you to learn about the world around you and will help you when studying. Allow this assistance to come to you naturally.

Now invoke the wisdom of archangel Jophiel who will render assistance with the realisation and development of your creative talents.

You will possess some form of creativity which you can harness for your own pleasure and contentment. Simply permit your creative talents to come to the fore and be fully realised as part of your healing journey. Take time out now to bring your appreciation of the beauty of the arts to full fruition.

Now turn your attention to the work of archangel Raphael whose special mission will be to assist you with healing your mind and your body when ailments strike.

Your goal will be to rid yourself of physical malaise and psychological distress and you can achieve this aim by beginning your journey of believing in yourself and your natural self-healing ability.

Archangel Chamuel can also assist you with relationship difficulties in order to restore harmony and peace in your life when you encounter troubled waters.

Perhaps a relationship in your life is unfruitful or detrimental and so major changes may need to occur before your personal energy has been drained completely?

Now invoke the healing energies of archangel Michael who will be there to protect you from unpleasantness, misfortunate and disturbing confrontation.

Archangel Michael can be your safety-belt and your invisible protective auric field against those people and situations which might seek to discomfort you. Invoke this assistance now and allow it to permeate your being.

Maybe you may wish to summon archangel Raziel into your sacred space when you need help with enhancing your insight and your perception?

You may sometimes feel that you have misunderstood what others say to you or the messages which you receive from the cosmos and so archangel Raziel will allow your psychic gifts to develop and assist you.

Archangel Zadkiel can also help you to become compassionate towards yourself and others who may be in need of your assistance.

Archangel Zadkiel will donate to you the empathy which you might need both for yourself and for those about you who are troubled. Your empathy will naturally develop the more your self-understanding and your self-wisdom grows during your own healing journey.

Now perhaps you can converse with archangel Haniel who will help you to reach your maximum potential in life and will assist you to become self-fulfilled in the process?

When you know that you are on the right path in life and that you have relinquished the dross then you will become your own person and can lead a rewarding life.

Archangel Metatron can be invoked if you are intending to assist others with their healing journey in a therapeutic capacity.

Archangel Metatron will give you the tools to assist others with their troubles, their pain and their suffering. If you wish to tread the path of the therapeutic practitioner then archangel Metatron will be your constant guide.

Now allow all the wisdom which you have gained about yourself both from your own mind and from the archangels with whom you have conversed to be integrated naturally into your soul.

Merely rest now and allow this enlightenment to be absorbed and captured forever.

Ensure that this wisdom has been fully accepted and then when you are completely ready and feel able to rejoin the outside world again then simply encourage yourself to drift back to full waking consciousness.

ASCENDED MASTERS

Do you believe that you have a dearth of personal inner wisdom?

Can you accept that you might find a helper who will travel with you along life's path?

Are you able to accept help and guidance from others as a matter of course?

WHAT IS AN ASCENDED MASTER?

The ascended masters will be spiritually enlightened beings who have previously incarnated on the earthly plane and, in doing so, have gained first-hand experience of the healing and enlightenment process (see Figure 16: *Ascended Masters*).

The ascended masters who will be particularly concerned with therapeutic healing will allow you to unfold your inner wisdom and to progress on your soul's journey.

There are an infinite number of ascended masters who can assist you in numerous way but there will be specific light beings who will be the most important for your unique healing journey.

FIGURE 16: ASCENDED MASTERS

ASCENDED MASTER	SYMBOLISM
El Morya Khan	Power Drive
Lord Lanto	Enlightenment Wisdom
Paul the Venetian	Love Compassion
Serapis Bey	Purity Harmony

Hilarion	Healing Abundance
Lady Nada	Humility Service
Saint Germain	Courage Freedom

EL MORYA KHAN

El Morya Khan will oversee your passage through life and your energetic drive which will propel you forward in order to create a fulfilled life for yourself. You can invoke the assistance of El Morya Khan, therefore, when you might feel despondent and lack motivation.

LORD LANTO

Lord Lanto will have a special mission to assist you with your personal enlightenment process and to develop your self-knowledge. You may wish to seek the help of Lord Lanto, therefore, when you are struggling to make sense of what your mind might be showing you and the confusion which might have been created in your life.

PAUL THE VENETIAN

Paul the Venetian will oversee the enhancement of your realistic self-concept and your fruitful relationships with others. You can invoke the assistance of Paul the Venetian, therefore, when you feel that you need to love yourself and to relinquish self-blame and self-punishment.

SERAPIS BAY

Serapis Bay will oversee your journey into personal peace and self-harmony when the conflict within your mind can be resolved. You can ask for help from Serapis Bay, therefore, so that you can unravel every aspect of your past distress which has arisen from your untoward life experiences.

Hilarion

Hilarion will assist you to expect and to reward yourself with abundance through self-healing. You might summon the assistance of Hilarion, therefore, so that you can value yourself and you can accept good fortunate as a normal part of your existence.

Lady Nada

Lady Nada will exist to allow you to become humble and non-judgemental towards others. You can invoke the power of Lady Nada, therefore, so that you can cease to blame others for your own distress which you might need to acknowledge rather than to externalise.

Saint Germain

Saint Germain will be the ascended master who will supervise you on your path towards emotive freedom and your mission to acquire the courage to act according to the dictates of your own mind. With the aid of Saint Germain, therefore, you can make your own choices in life and stand on your own two feet in the storm.

Ascended masters therapeutic text

Settle into the depths of your inner mind as the key to all cosmic order and creation.

Allow the power and strength of cosmic energy to encompass you and enfold you.

Feel the power of the universe working in your own interests in order to help you to relax.

Today you can make contact with those light beings who exist to assist your healing journey through this lifetime and many other lifetimes.

Perhaps you wish to enhance your personal power and your ability to be interested in life and motivated towards attaining your goals?

You can invoke the power and wisdom of El Morya Khan whose special mission will be to assist you in order to attain and to lead a fulfilled and energy-packed life.

You might also wish to summon Lord Lanto who will be delighted to help you to become more and more enlightened in order to provide you with inner wisdom.

Lord Lanto can turn the key for you so that you can look inwardly and consider those experiences in your life which have caused you unnecessary distress. You can also gain help with being tolerant and compassionate towards yourself with Lord Lanto's encouragement.

Paul the Venetian can be invoked in order to assist you with loving and valuing yourself so that you can be understanding of others and thus your personal relationships will improve from this vantage point.

In your quest for purity and harmony within your psyche you might wish to summon the assistance of Serapis Bay.

You might require the help of Serapis Bay if you feel that you are sometimes inadequate, undeserving or lacking in confidence because of the way in which you have been unfairly treated by others in the past.

You can, of course, give healing to yourself with the help of Hilarion who will encourage you to accept yourself and the fact that those things which you seek can be attained naturally.

Perhaps you can acknowledge your own failings but, in addition, truthfully apportion blame to those who have wronged you in the past rather than remaining self-effacing and blaming yourself?

Lady Nada can assist you to be humble enough to accept the help of those about you who are genuinely interested in your welfare.

You might find yourself shunning the company of others who simply make demands on you and drain your energy. But you can become non-judgmental of others by looking inwardly and honestly at your own life and those around you.

Now let yourself summon the aid of Saint Germain who can speed you on your way towards emotive freedom and contentment.

Saint Germain's special mission will be to propel you forward towards true self-enlightenment which will stand you in your stead for many lifetimes.

Give yourself the gift of enlightenment by contacting these ascended masters and bringing their powerful wisdom into your life.

Know that this process of spiritual progression will need very little encouragement from you and will occur naturally as your go about your daily business.

But for now permit yourself to return into the present moment knowing that you have attained a valuable lesson which will assist you on your ongoing healing journey.

Simply enjoy the peace for the rest of your life because you have worked hard and can be granted the gift of peace and enlightenment as a result of all your efforts and determination.

LORDS OF KARMA

Do you believe that you have a backlog of unresolved karma?

Can you stop believing that you are to blame for everything which has occurred in your life?

Are you willing to accept that your untoward past can be resolved, demystified and diminished to insignificance?

WHAT IS A LORD OF KARMA?

The lords of karma will be ascended masters who, in metaphysical philosophy, are the keepers of the akashic records of the etheric plane (see Figure 17: *Lords of Karma*).

The akashic records will document your karmic history, your soul's evolution and your future aspirations.

Each lord of karma has a special mission within a special spiritual committee in order to orchestrate the divine plan for the cosmos. You could thus think of each office of the lords of karma as fulfilling a mission rather like a board of directors of an organisation.

The offices of the various lords of karma will be occupied by spiritually enlightened beings who will take on the roles of president, managing director and other board directors with special responsibility for motivation, liberty, wisdom, integrity, intelligence, healing and justice within the universe.

You can invite the lords of karma collectively to assist you to banish your karmic history and to facilitate your healing evolution and empowerment so that you can progress and flourish.

FIGURE 17: LORDS OF KARMA

LORD	MISSION	SYMBOLISM
Great divine director	Master of divine plan	Power Drive

Goddess of liberty	Chairperson of the lords	Freedom Equality
Lady Nada	Voice of silence	Purity Wisdom
Pallas Athena	Goddess of truth	Integrity Truth
Cyclopea	Creator of gods	Intellect Communication
Kwan Yin	Goddess of compassion	Healing Transformation
Lady Portia	Goddess of justice	Judgement Equality

GREAT DIVINE DIRECTOR

The great divine director will be the equivalent of the president of the board of the lords of karma. The great divine director will, therefore, oversee your ability to motivate yourself with action, energy, power and drive in order to realise your ambitions and to achieve your chosen goals in life.

GODDESS OF LIBERTY

The goddess of liberty will be the equivalent of the chairman and the managing director of the board of the lords of karma. The goddess of liberty will, therefore, oversee your ability to set yourself free from distress and will help you to regard yourself as equal to others instead of feeling inferior to everyone whom you meet.

LADY NADA

Lady Nada will be responsible for allowing humanity to look inwardly in silent contemplation. Lady Nada will, therefore, oversee your ability to purify your soul with therapeutic intervention and self-healing in order to gain your inner wisdom.

PALLAS ATHENA

Pallas Athena will be responsible for allowing humanity to seek personal truth and integrity. Pallas Athena will, therefore, oversee your ability to understand your soul with therapeutic intervention and self-healing so that you can be honest with yourself and can discover your personal truth.

CYCLOPEA

Cyclopea will be responsible for allowing humanity to gain intellectual knowledge and understanding of the world. Cyclopea will, therefore, oversee your ability to learn skills for your chosen occupation and to study information for leisure-time pursuits.

KWAN YIN

Kwan Yin will be responsible for allowing humanity to seek therapeutic intervention in order to overcome distress and unhappiness. Kwan Yin will, therefore, oversee your ability to obtain the appropriate therapeutic intervention and self-healing which will enable you to forgive yourself for any perceived misdeeds or inaction.

LADY PORTIA

Lady Portia will be responsible for allowing humanity to obtain justice and freedom of speech in order to encourage those with unresolved karma to complete their healing journey appropriately. Lady Portia will, therefore, oversee your ability to progress through therapeutic intervention and self-healing in order to allow you to rid yourself of karmic troubles and setbacks.

LORDS OF KARMA THERAPEUTIC TEXT

Permit yourself some time and space so that you can devote your attention to furthering your healing mission.

Simply relax knowing that your focus on your inner mind will allow you to unravel and to resolve your dilemmas naturally and effortlessly.

Everything which has caused you distress in the past will have taken its toll and will have had a lasting impact on you.

The more you investigate your past untoward experience the more you will be able to release the emotive negativity which has beset you and dragged you down.

Perhaps you could look at those aspects of your past which have caused you the greatest distress, unhappiness and even regret?

Maybe you can sift and sort through your memory-bank in order to identify those experiences which have troubled you the most and will have left a legacy of unhappiness and problems in their wake?

Do you lack motivation and drive because you feel that life is simply not worth living?

Do you feel that you have been unfairly treated or that you are in an inescapable trap in your life?

Do you consider that you lack self-wisdom and are beset by confusion as a result?

Are you able to see life realistically and to discover your personal truth?

Can you let go of logical thinking in favour of exploring your inner mind?

Can you further the process of unravelling your distressful past?

Can you now apportion blame on those who have treated you unfairly without making too many excuses for those who have wronged you?

Once you have identified and excavated in detail those events and occurrences currently lodged in your inner mind which have had a lasting effect on you and which have had a knock-on effect into the present you will be able to move forward in life.

Now perhaps you can be assisted by the lords of karma who will be able to help you to banish the effects of the past and the legacy which you have been carrying around with you?

Simply ask the lords of karma to assist you to banish your demons and to free yourself from those untoward experiences which have affected you deeply and have caused you great suffering.

Your pain will not last forever and cannot dominate your life once you have investigated your troubles, spoken about them honestly and released the underlying emotive suffering which your experiences have engendered.

Once you feel that you have relinquished some of your karmic history then perhaps you can content yourself with the knowledge that you can in future consult the lords of karma as necessary?

Now invite yourself to drift back into the present having gained much inner wisdom and enlightenment which will put a new spring in your step and lighten your spirits.

Shamanic Healing

SHAMANIC HEALING

The value of shamanic healing will be to enable you to make contact with vibrational beings from the natural world.

Shamanic healing will permit you to imaginatively reach and invoke the assistance of healing agents in the guise of power spirits.

SHAMANIC HEALING PRACTICE

Have you discovered that you have an inherent affinity with the natural world?

Are you able to appreciate the power and majesty of the natural world which surrounds you?

Can you observe nature in the raw and marvel at its potency and grace?

WHAT IS SHAMANIC HEALING?

Shamanic healing will be a therapeutic process which will allow you to access the world of nature spirits in a meditative state in order to meet your spirit helpers and your spiritual teachers so that you can further your healing journey (see Figure 18: *Shamanic Healing*).

If you consult a shamanic healer your practitioner may enter a hypnotic state in order to guide you through a number of processes using techniques, such as drumming or chanting, which will assist you with shamanic journeying and soul retrieval. Shamanic journeying will enable you to meet your spirit guides and your spiritual teachers and shamanic soul retrieval will assist you to heal your soul's fragmentation as a direct result of stressful or traumatic experience in your life.

The practice of shamanic healing originated with the native American culture when the shaman was the medicine man who performed ceremonial rituals when tending the sick within an indigenous community.

FIGURE 18: SHAMANIC HEALING

SHAMANIC JOURNEYING	SHAMANIC SOUL RETRIEVAL
Meetings spirit guides & teachers	Healing soul fragmentation

SHAMANIC JOURNEYING

Are you willing to accept assistance from a shamanic power spirit?

Do you feel an affinity with another mythic creature other than one from the human species?

Would you like to explore the concept of adopting a powerful animal spirit who could assist you with your healing voyage?

WHAT IS SHAMANIC JOURNEYING?

Shamanic journeying will allow you to forge your healing path towards self-knowledge and self-enlightenment by contacting your personal power animals and your spiritual teachers in line with native American medical practice (see Figure 19: *Shamanic Journeying*).

Your shamanic journey will allow you to symbolically leave the earth plane via the middle world which represents a hypnotic state in order to visit archetypal spirit guides in the lower world and spiritual teachers in the upper world.

A shamanic journey to the lower world of spirit guides will empower you to excavate your origins and to encounter and greet your power animal or other mythic creature.

A shamanic journey to the upper world will allow you to visit a higher plane within your mind in order to find your spiritual teachers. Your spiritual teachers can empower you to become more self-aware and to attain self-enlightenment.

FIGURE 19: SHAMANIC JOURNEYING

LOWER WORLD	MIDDLE WORLD	UPPER WORLD
Meeting spirit guides	Hypnotic state	Meeting spiritual teachers

SHAMANIC GUIDES AND TEACHERS

Shamanic journeying will be a means of meeting your spirit guides and your spiritual teachers who can assist you not only with your healing journey but also with daily life (see Figure 20: *Shamanic Guides and Teachers*).

Shamanic healing when combined with native American medicine wheel practice can highlight a power animal or a spiritual teacher who can focus you on various aspects of your healing journey. Within native American healing traditions four specific power animals are associated with the elements and the seasons.

You can utilise shamanic healing practice yourself by invoking the power of spirit animals or spiritual teachers who can assist you personally. A shamanic power animal guide or teacher can also assist you when you are helping others to heal.

You can select your unique shamanic power animal guide or wise teacher who will accompany you on your therapeutic journey and, of course, your choice can be made from the entire spectrum of the animal kingdom and the natural world.

FIGURE 20: SHAMANIC GUIDES AND TEACHERS

DIRECTION	ELEMENT	SEASON	POWER ANIMAL	SYMBOLISM
North	Air	Spring	Eagle	Intellectual state Birth Empathy
South	Water	Winter	Bear	Emotional state Adulthood Self-love
East	Fire	Summer	Wolf	Energetic state Youth Generosity

West	Earth	Autumn	Buffalo	Physical state Maturity Compassion

EAGLE

The eagle in shamanic philosophy will symbolise your mental state and the air qualities of the north. The north in shamanic healing practice will be symbolic of spring, birth and empathy with others.

BEAR

The bear in shamanic philosophy will symbolise your emotional state and the water qualities of the south. The south in shamanic healing practice will be symbolic of winter, adulthood and self-love.

WOLF

The wolf in shamanic philosophy will symbolise your energetic state and the fire qualities of the east. The east in shamanic healing practice will be symbolic of summer, youth and gratitude at being alive.

BUFFALO

The buffalo in shamanic philosophy will symbolise your physical state and the earth qualities of the west. The west in shamanic healing practice will be symbolic of autumn, maturity and compassion towards humanity.

SHAMANIC JOURNEYING THERAPEUTIC TEXT

Give yourself time and space to relax and think inwardly in a meditative state of mind and a relaxed physical state.

You may wish to make contact with those animal spirits or mythic creatures from the natural world who can assist you on your path towards freedom and enlightenment.

Could you take yourself on an imaginary journey through a forest which has a distinct path running through it and yet as you go through the woodland it may be dark and dense?

But you may still be able to see the sunlight shafting through the leaves of the trees which are silhouetted against the sky. This sunlight, even if it is meagre, can still light your way through the dark forest. You will, by this means, be able to make out the path in front of you through the dense woodland.

You will be able to smell the bark of the trees and the forest flowers beneath your feet.

You will be able to listen to the birds or the cries of the wild creatures here.

Can you hear the rustle of the leaves and feel a gentle breeze as you walk onward?

The further you walk the more you will be able to see your path through the thick woodland.

Perhaps you can even notice that your path is sloping gently upward towards a high mountain or downward to the bank of a vibrant river?

Pause here to behold the beauty and the majesty of nature in the raw.

Now will be the time for you to meet your spirit animal guide or your wise teacher who will help you to heal by bringing you peace.

You may need to look within the forest itself or by the riverside. You may wish to view your power animal guide or your spiritual teacher by climbing to the top of the mountain.

Your mind will show you which way to look and to wait until your spirit animal guide or your spiritual teacher comes into view to greet you.

Your special spirit guide or teacher may, of course, be a living creature, such as an animal, a bird or a fish, or it could also be an imaginary creature from myth or legend or simply a being from your own imagination.

Now introduce yourself to your spirit animal guide or spiritual teacher and get to know your new lifetime companion who will assist you always in your endeavours and particularly in times of difficulty.

Spend some time now conversing with your unique spirit guide or your spiritual teacher and allow this communication to assist you, to enlighten you and to guide you on your way.

Garner all this wisdom into your soul and when you feel that you have accomplished your mission for today then allow yourself to trickle back into the physical world and your familiar surroundings.

SHAMANIC SOUL RETRIEVAL

Do you feel that your soul has been fragmented as a result of any unpleasant past experience?

Do you feel somehow lost within yourself?

Are you able to concede that your soul can be made whole with some assistance from the natural world?

What is shamanic soul retrieval?

Shamanic soul retrieval will provide you with a means of rescuing yourself from the rigours of life's distress.

Shamanic soul retrieval will help you to heal fragmented parts of your psyche which have endured pain and suffering as a result of stress, shock and trauma. You will almost certainly have encountered experiences which have caused you to dissociate from your physical body as an out-of-body experience when you might have lost control in a given situation and were forced to relinquish your own personal power.

Soul retrieval, consequently, will empower you to recapture your fragmented self and to smooth out the devastation which past experiences will have engendered for you.

Shamanic soul retrieval therapeutic text

Why not find that part of you which wishes to be released from the pain and anguish of your suffering?

Ask yourself to relax fully and to sink into the realm of enquiry and soul-searching in a way which is right for you and for you alone.

Sometimes you may find that you stand apart from the crowd perhaps?

Or maybe you feel isolated from yourself and from society?

Might you have lost an aspect of yourself which suddenly can become out of control when you least want this to happen because it causes you to panic and to fret?

Maybe you lose your temper far too easily or you start to quake when you try to speak?

Do you sometimes feel that you cannot grasp and retain your personal power and that you feel out of control most of the time because you are at the mercy of your own negative emotive reactions?

Might you feel that you are very depressed or that you are not really here with your feet on the ground on occasion?

When there is a part of you which somehow feels different or detached from the true you it will be time for you to retrieve that aspect of your soul which has become disjointed, out of step or fragmented in some way.

Let yourself travel to another realm where you can locate that lost part of yourself.

Perhaps you felt lost many years ago?

Maybe you were a child or a young person who did not know what the world had to offer?

Were you at the mercy of your parents, your guardians, your schoolteachers or your compatriots in the past?

Just take some time out now to discover when you were first lost to yourself.

When did you first feel that life had evaded you and that you had lost control of your feelings and your senses?

Locate that distressed part of you with a view to showing yourself some love and understanding in the unpleasant situation or circumstances in which you found yourself back then.

Now will be the time to summon your spirit guide or your spiritual teacher who will assist you to heal the past and to resolve your pain and suffering.

Perhaps you can talk to that little part of yourself?

Maybe you could caress and nurture yourself by drying your tears and giving yourself comfort?

Could you bring some understanding to the situation which you are revisiting and re-examining?

Could you find a creative way of helping yourself to come to terms with your past experiences and your past suffering as a means of retrieving your lost soul?

Ask your spirit guides and spiritual teachers to assist you in the best way possible.

Now ask yourself whether the past can be laid to rest while you continue along your life's path.

When you feel that you have achieved this great task for yourself it will be time to congratulate yourself on your accomplishments before you return to the everyday world.

Empower yourself to emerge into a new world which you can behold with enlightenment and appreciation.

Tarot

TAROT

The value of tarot will be to enable you to contemplate your healing journey in terms of symbolism.

Tarot imagery will permit you to imaginatively explore your life and your worldly existence.

TAROT PRACTICE

Do you appreciate that life's journey can be full of ups and downs?

Can you see the therapeutic value of contemplating the symbolism of your life's journey?

Are you aware that your life as a whole and in parts will be a total picture?

WHAT IS TAROT?

The tarot will provide you with a means of understanding your life's mission and your existential voyage which can be interpreted via archetypal imagery (see Figure 21: *Tarot*).

The tarot pack will consist of seventy-eight cards which are divided into the major arcana and the minor arcana.

The twenty-two cards of the major arcana will symbolically depict your major life events.

The fifty-six cards of the minor arcana will metaphorically represent your day-to-day activity.

The tarot cards are used as a form of predictive divination but when employed judiciously can represent a rich abundance of symbolism which will assist you to understand yourself and your psyche.

FIGURE 21: TAROT

MAJOR ARCANA	MINOR ARCANA
Major life events 22 cards	Day-to-day activity 56 cards

MAJOR ARCANA

Do you realise the way in which your life transits a number of lengthy and important phases?

Do you consider that you are on a spiritual journey throughout your life?

Are you aware that your childhood was a journey into adulthood?

WHAT IS THE MAJOR ARCANA?

The twenty-two cards of the major arcana will symbolically depict your major life events which can have a profound impact on your spiritual development and your personal evolution (see Figure 22: *Major Arcana*).

The therapeutic significance of the major arcana will be to enable you to trace a significant episode in your life as if you were undertaking a journey from birth to maturity. You can utilise the imagery contained within the major arcana in order to encourage your spirit to unfold by visualising your healing journey. You can also extract cards from the major arcana in order to guide yourself forward from your current life position.

Because you will be utilising tarot symbolism in a therapeutic context within psycho-spiritual therapy you would be advised not to read the cards with any negative connotation. You can in this way employ the tarot principally as a means of unravelling the conflict in your soul.

If you intend to purchase a tarot pack then ensure that you select a pack with imagery which appeals strongly and directly to you because this will tell you much about yourself which you might wish to discover.

FIGURE 22: MAJOR ARCANA

NUMBER	NAME	SYMBOLISM
0	The fool	Beginning a new venture, enterprise or phase of your life
1	The magician	Trusting in your personal resources, talents and attributes

2	The high priestess	Awakening your emotive and spiritual nature
3	The empress	Awakening your feminine and nurturing nature
4	The emperor	Awakening your masculine and self-assertive nature
5	The hierophant	Consulting your spiritual wisdom and inner self
6	The lovers	Acknowledging opposing elements and taking important decisions
7	The chariot	Harnessing a number of diverse elements
8	Strength	Realising your personal inner strength and determination
9	The hermit	Resting and withdrawing from the turmoil of life
10	The wheel of fortune	Appreciating the peaks and troughs of life
11	Justice	Searching for your personal truth and integrity
12	The hanged man	Deciding to make a conscious self-sacrifice for the benefit of another
13	Death	Changing irrevocably for the better
14	Temperance	Ensuring balance and moderation
15	The devil	Examining your inner mind and soul
16	The tower	Breaking down restrictions and barriers to beneficial change
17	The star	Realising your hopes and aspirations
18	The moon	Realising your emotive life and intuition
19	The sun	Realising your personal goals and achievements

20	Judgement	Reversing your misfortune and gaining reward for your spiritual endeavour
21	The world	Completing a major project in your life

MAJOR ARCANA THERAPEUTIC TEXT

Allow yourself to enter a relaxed state of mind in which you can communicate with your inner self.

Your inner self knows everything about you which you might not yet have discovered consciously.

Maybe you could consider the symbolism contained within the major arcana of the tarot?

The symbolism of the tarot will hold the key to the unwinding of your inner self.

The journey inherent within the major arcana of the tarot will begin with your birth.

Set your imagination free and allow yourself to visualise what life was like on the day you were born.

Ask yourself how you felt when you were born and how those around you felt and thought about your arrival?

Consider whether you approached life in this world with optimism and good expectations or whether you felt dismal about the prospect of life?

Your introduction into this world was a time of naivety and innocence when you were a babe in arms as reported by the fool in your tarot pack.

But consider what you brought into this world in the guise of your inner magician?

You had all your talents and personal resources with you when you were born and these attributes simply needed to be recognised and developed.

The magician in your life is the one who unleashes all your personal attributes which will have been inherent within you from the moment of your birth.

But perhaps you may not have recognised your personal attributes?

Give yourself permission now to acknowledge your inherent talents.

Now perhaps you can consider the high priestess within you who symbolises your spiritual nature and your psychic life which were also present even from the early days of your life?

The high priestess calls on you to acknowledge your negative emotive reactions to your life's unpleasant experiences and she invites you to overcome your pain and suffering by revisiting and releasing any distress from the past.

The empress within you will allow your nurturing qualities to unfold as an acknowledgement of the feminine side of your nature which seeks to come to the fore.

The emperor will show you your powerful and self-assertive nature as the balancing agent which will permit you to become a fully rounded being comprising both the feminine and the masculine qualities which will make you a whole person.

Have you yet acknowledged these qualities which have been sitting dormant within you for some time?

Next maybe you can consult the hierophant who will bring you the realisation of your spiritual identity which contains your self-knowledge and your inner wisdom and which will be constantly evolving within you?

Now allow yourself to examine those opposing elements of your nature which can cause confusion and even conflict within you because you are a whole being. Sometimes these opposing factors will come from within you or these elements may be outside your control because of circumstances.

These opposing elements which are depicted in the lovers in the tarot may even mean that you will need to take an important decision or to choose between two extremes.

The chariot card will prove to you that you do have everything which you might need in order to organise your life and to bring together all the threads of your existence so that you can restore balance.

Next the strength card will show you that you do have inner strength and resilience within your nature in order to withstand anything which life may toss your way.

You might need to apply the wisdom of the hermit who will request that you withdraw from the hubbub of life in order to afford yourself time and space for healing and contemplation.

Could you also consider that the wheel of fortune may turn at one time in your favour but the next minute the downturn may not be so favourable?

Empower yourself to accept that life consists of ups and downs and that the turmoil will eventually come to rest in order to maintain the status quo for you.

You may have a need to search for personal truth and to uphold your integrity at times which will be symbolised by the justice card in your tarot pack. Justice will empower you to be true to yourself and not to lose control of your personal power.

Sometimes the symbolism of the hanged man may be an important factor in your life when you consciously elect to make a self-sacrifice in the interests of doing the right thing for the benefit of others or those who depend on you for their existence.

Now maybe you can reflect on the symbolism of death and the rebirth which will be brought in its wake?

Sometimes you might know deep inside that inevitable and beneficial change will and must happen in order to allow you to move forward in life. You should welcome such events as a growth experience from which you will benefit in a special way.

The temperance card requests that you find a workable balance in your existence so that you can apply moderation when life looks and feels as if it is turning a summersault.

Perhaps you can examine your life in order to discover this process of balance at work?

Next you can consider the devil within you who may keep nagging away at you in order to encourage you to examine your personal thoughts and feelings which lie deep within your soul.

The devil within your tarot pack will open the door for you to experience deep healing and to gain personal enlightenment in the process.

Could you now see the tower card in front of you which signifies that you and your life may need to make an irreversible and irrevocable change for the better?

The tower will remove any barriers which might have been constructed and yet were actually unnecessary and are now utterly redundant.

Now allow yourself to excavate your hopes and aspirations about the present and the future with the star in your tarot.

Could you permit yourself to dare to hope to bring yourself good fortune and abundance?

These cosmic gifts can soon be realised once you have acknowledged your wishes, your dreams and your self-worth.

The moon in your tarot pack represents the realisation of your emotive life and the resolution of your negative patterning once you have examined your own psyche and have worked through your distress.

The sun will similarly enable you to realise your personal goals and to acknowledge your achievements as a result of your healing journey and your personal effort.

If you consider the symbolism of judgement you will soon be able to appreciate that there are times in your life when the results of your efforts will inevitably mean that your ill-fortune and your distress can be resolved and rectified.

Finally the card representing the world will show you that you can lead the kind of existence which will be most beneficial for you and which will be the result of your life experience, inner wisdom and personal endeavour.

So now you can simply allow your mind to undergo its transformation and to know that you are on a path of self-learning.

And once you have absorbed all these thoughts and feelings then simply return to the present moment as a newly enlightened being.

MINOR ARCANA

Do you frequently feel burdened with the minutiae of day-to-day life?

Can you simultaneously focus on the wider picture and the detail?

Are you beset by a negative situation which will eventually resolve naturally?

WHAT IS THE MINOR ARCANA?

The fifty-six cards of the minor arcana will symbolically depict your day-to-day activity as your life unfolds (see Figure 23: *Minor Arcana*).

The minor arcana will be sub-divided into four suits of rods, pentacles, swords and cups. Each of the four suits of rods, pentacles, swords and cups of the minor arcana will symbolically be associated with one of the four elements of fire, earth, air and water.

Each of the four suits will consist of fourteen cards which will symbolically represent the main components of your psyche, your physicality and your existence.

Each minor arcana suit will comprise ten standard cards and four court cards.

The therapeutic significance of the minor arcana will be that you can monitor a short phase in your life which will allow you to move forward by overcoming minor setbacks from which you can gain personal enlightenment about your existence as life unfolds for you. You will be provided with an opportunity to learn about yourself, to develop your relationship with others and to overcome challenges in life with the assistance of the minor arcana.

The minor arcana will hold therapeutic value in terms of its symbolism of those factors with which you may need to contend on a daily basis. The minor arcana will empower you to discover the way in which your self-regard, your relationship with others and your reaction to circumstances can be guided by your inner resources because the substance of your inner mind will be reflected in the world about you.

Figure 23: Minor Arcana

Rods	Pentacles	Swords	Cups
Energy resources Fire element	Financial resources Earth element	Mental resources Air element	Emotive resources Water element

Rods

The suit of rods (or wands) in the minor arcana will be symbolic of your energy resources, your creativity and your active imagination.

The rods in the minor arcana will be associated with the symbolism of the fire element.

You will need to assess your energy levels and your motivation in life in order to marshal the resources which you will need for your survival.

The therapeutic value of the rods in the minor arcana will be to enlighten you about your personal attributes and your motivational drive which will highlight your enthusiasm and your determination to overcome any obstacles which might be strewn in your path.

Pentacles

The suit of pentacles (or coins) in the minor arcana will be symbolic of your finances, your possessions and your business acumen.

The pentacles in the minor arcana will be associated with the symbolism of the earth element.

You will need to handle your monetary resources and your personal wealth and, perhaps more importantly, to consider your relationship with your personal possessions and assets.

The therapeutic value of the pentacles in the minor arcana will be to enlighten you about your monetary resources and your personal possessions which will assist you to attain security and stability in your existence.

Swords

The suit of swords in the minor arcana will be symbolic of your cognition, your intellect and your communication skills.

The swords in the minor arcana will be associated with the symbolism of the air element.

You will need to examine your thoughts on a daily basis and to note your negative reactions to people and to circumstances.

The therapeutic value of the swords in the minor arcana will be to enlighten you about your inner negative thoughts and your limiting beliefs which may impede you as you progress through life.

Cups

The suit of cups in the minor arcana will be symbolic of your emotive resources, your intuition and your ability to form fruitful relationships.

The cups in the minor arcana will be associated with the symbolism of the water element.

You will need to consider your emotive reactions and your uncontrollable negative responses to people and to circumstances.

The therapeutic value of the cups in the minor arcana will be to enlighten you about your inner feelings and your distressful reactions which may hold you back from attaining contentment.

Minor arcana standard cards

The ten standard cards in each suit of the minor arcana will symbolically depict a journey during which your relationship with yourself and your life circumstances can be examined (see Figure 24: *Minor Arcana Standard Cards*).

FIGURE 24: MINOR ARCANA STANDARD CARDS

NUMBER	SYMBOLISM
Ace	Starting a new phase of your life
Two	Assessing your prospects
Three	Planning for your future
Four	Visualising your future
Five	Foreseeing any potential obstacles
Six	Striving for your goals
Seven	Overcoming any obstacles
Eight	Taking stock of your existence
Nine	Realising your efforts
Ten	Bringing your project to fruition

MINOR ARCANA COURT CARDS

The court cards of the minor arcana will show you an aspect of yourself and the influence of others in your life (see Figure 25: *Minor Arcana Court Cards*).

The four court cards will consist of the page, the knight, the queen and the king in each suit.

The page will symbolically represent the naivety and the trusting nature of childhood.

The knight will symbolically represent the resourcefulness and the enterprising nature of adolescence.

The queen will symbolically represent the intuition and the wisdom of adulthood.

The king will symbolically represent the knowledge and the success of maturity.

FIGURE 25: MINOR ARCANA COURT CARDS

CARD	SYMBOLISM	ELEMENT
Page	Your inner awareness Influence of naive and trusting people Childhood	Earth
Knight	Your inner resources Influence of resourceful and enterprising people Adolescence	Fire
Queen	Your inner aspirations Influence of intuitive and wise people Adulthood	Water
King	Your inner potential Influence of knowledgeable and successful people Maturity	Air

MINOR ARCANA THERAPEUTIC TEXT

Relax into yourself and permit yourself to enter a phase of contemplation. Let your inner mind step away from the hustle and bustle of life and put aside those tasks and thoughts which would normally demand your attention.

Reflect on your energy resources to see if you are really pulling your weight in life and helping yourself to move forward.

Do you have the determination to succeed or do you accept failure with equanimity?

Are you lacking in motivation because you feel that your efforts will be wasted?

Are you killing yourself with overwork because you feel that you must keep on striving?

Do you have a failure-button encrusted in your soul?

Search for a means of balancing your working-time with your leisure-time.

Find the key to realising your dreams without draining your energy resources. Take the first step now to realising your full potential.

Now might also be the time to reflect on the state of your finances and to consider what assets you possess?

Look to see if you regard yourself as rich or poor.

Can you consider whether your monetary resources are overstretched and whether you are living beyond your means?

You might alternatively believe that you are undeserving and so do not have the right to accept or to accumulate wealth.

Or you might even consider that you have too much money and, therefore, you should give it all away and deprive yourself unnecessarily.

Perhaps you hold many desires and yet these cannot be obtained through a lack of funds and this fact saddens you?

Whatever your relationship with wealth and abundance you might need to take a long hard look at your fortune or your misfortune and consider how it makes you feel.

If you have sufficient monetary resources can you resolve to accept your good fortune and to spend your money wisely rather than frittering it away on meaningless luxury?

If you have insufficient finances and are struggling to keep your head above water can you now find a way of examining the reasons why you feel undeserving or discover a way in which you can summon wealth into your life?

Just allow this process to subsume you so that a solution can be readily found.

Also ensure that you remove from your life anyone who might be an obstacle to your progress. If there is someone in your life who is draining your financial resources then banish these impediments from your existence and subsequently invite into your life those who are truly on your side.

Allow yourself at this point to consider how your thoughts about yourself and your life have impacted on your outlook.

Do you have a negative outlook on life and feel despondent about your lot?

Or could you be hampered by unrealistic thoughts of danger which surrounds you?

Do you feel that life is a constant struggle and that you are continually losing the battle?

Are you held back by your doubts and uncertainties about your own ability?

Can you take time out now to consider the origin of your trepidation and find an ingenious means of resolving the impasse?

Can you dig your way out of the morass which burdens your mind and lighten the load for yourself now with some creative thinking?

Urge yourself forward in order to brighten your future and set your mind free.

Empower yourself by bringing into your life others who are supportive and whom you can trust rather than fraternising with unhelpful people who scheme to trip you up constantly.

Can you now turn your thoughts to your emotive reactions in order to excavate your mind?

Might you be beset with doubts and worries about the future?

Are you weighed down by irrational fears and anxieties?

Do you feel unrealistically guilty about something which you feel was all your fault?

Do you feel that even getting out of bed is a struggle because you feel so downhearted and lost?

Might you feel perpetually in the depths of midwinter in your soul with no spring flowers on the horizon?

Do you feel the loss of a loved one who has deserted you?

Can you allow your mind to return to those times in your life when you were most distressed, forlorn and scared and consider the impact which these events have had on your feelings?

Perhaps you can satisfactorily resolve any past unhappiness or danger by reliving and redrafting the unhappy events in your memory?

Could you rectify a wrong or an injustice creatively and imaginatively?

Find a foolproof way of relieving yourself of unwarranted guilt and banish it to insignificance.

Allow yourself to fully experience and release your emotive pain and suffering.

Now you can attract helpful and loving people into your existence so that you can lead the happy and fulfilled life which you richly deserve.

Spend time now allowing all your thoughts and feelings to settle and look forward to a brighter and more productive future which will inspire you and bring you well-deserved happiness.

Bring yourself back into the now moment only when you feel that you have done your work for today in this very special place in your mind.

Simply allow yourself to drift back to today safe in the knowledge that you have healed a vital part of yourself and have taken a very important step on your journey towards recovery so that you can lead a full and fruitful life.

Welcome yourself back into today with a feeling that you have achieved many things for yourself in a very short space of time and that this progress will continue unaided from now on.

ASTROLOGY

ASTROLOGY

The value of astrology will be to enable you to contemplate your character traits, your inclinations, your motivations and your healing journey.

Astrology will permit you to understand yourself at a deeper cosmic level.

ASTROLOGICAL PRACTICE

Do you appreciate the value of understanding yourself implicitly?

Have you looked at yourself from a number of juxtaposed angles?

Could you assist yourself greatly with self-understanding?

WHAT IS ASTROLOGY?

Astrology will provide you with a means of understanding yourself and your relationship to the grand cosmic scheme which can be interpreted via the archetypal imagery of zodiac signs, planetary signs and astrological houses (see Figure 26: *Astrology*).

The symbolic imagery inherent within astrological interpretation will assess your personality traits through the position of the planetary signs as each transits through the zodiac signs and through the astrological houses at the moment of your birth. This information will usually be recorded using an astrological natal chart (or birth chart) format.

The zodiac signs will symbolically examine your personality traits and your personal inclinations.

The planetary signs will denote the external influences which are brought to bear on the zodiac signs in your natal chart.

The astrological houses will, furthermore, specify those areas of your existence which will be affected by the position of the planets transiting the zodiac signs in your natal chart.

You may need to find an internet-based source which will furnish you with your natal chart data provided that you know your date of birth, time of birth and place of birth. You may even wish to invest in some commercial software in order to explore these topics in more depth.

Figure 26: Astrology

Sign	Planet	House
Character traits	External influences	Life spheres

EXOTERIC-ESOTERIC ASTROLOGY

Do you realise that your outer persona and your inner psyche may be in conflict?

Would you consider that you are currently resolving your dilemmas from below the surface of your existence?

Can you appreciate the value of looking inwardly at yourself?

WHAT IS EXOTERIC-ESOTERIC ASTROLOGY?

There are two approaches to astrological interpretation in the guise of exoteric astrology (or personality-centred astrology) and esoteric astrology (or soul-centred astrology) both of which can assist you therapeutically (see Figure 27: *Esoteric and Exoteric Astrology*).

Both exoteric and esoteric astrology will collectively retain therapeutic value into which you can easily tap. Exoteric astrology will permit you to see the influence of your life's hazards and experiences as an outer effect while esoteric astrology will empower you to focus on resolving your underlying dilemmas as an inner cause.

The transition from exoteric astrology towards esoteric philosophy will reflect the current age and a growing awareness of life below the superficial surface of human existence.

FIGURE 27: ESOTERIC AND EXOTERIC ASTROLOGY

EXOTERIC ASTROLOGY	ESOTERIC ASTROLOGY
Personality evolution Outer effect Sun-sign focus	Soul evolution Inner cause Ascendant-sign focus

EXOTERIC ASTROLOGY

Exoteric astrology will empower you to consider your character traits and those factors which will contribute to any difficulties which you may have in terms of your relationship with yourself and with others as the effect of your inner distress.

Because exoteric astrology will deal principally with your character traits you will largely be considering the effects of your untoward life experience. Exoteric astrology will aim at the integration of your personality as its highest goal so that imbalances within your mind, body, cognitive faculties and emotive responses can be brought into harmony.

The main focus of exoteric astrology will be your sun sign (or star sign) as that zodiac sign which the sun was transiting at the moment of your birth. Exoteric astrology will place importance on your sun sign as your inherent personality indicator.

Exoteric astrology is often associated with the former age of Pisces which transpired when the vernal equinox entered the constellation of Pisces according to metaphysical philosophy. The Piscean age symbolically represents the Middle Ages when staunch religious practice dominated current debate and philosophy.

ESOTERIC ASTROLOGY

Esoteric astrology will empower you to consider your soul's evolutionary journey through life and will be concerned with the root-cause of any dilemmas with which you may be beset rather than with the effect itself.

Because esoteric astrology will deal principally with your soul's evolutionary journey you will largely be considering the causes of your psychological malaise which have resulted from your untoward life experiences. Esoteric astrology will aim at the integration of your psyche and the fulfilment of your potential as your healing mission.

The main focus of esoteric astrology will be your ascendant sign (or rising sign) as that zodiac sign which appeared on the eastern horizon at the moment of your birth. Esoteric astrology will emphasise the importance of your ascendant sign as the prime mover within your inner psyche and the means by which you will find the key to resolving distress within your soul.

Esoteric astrology will essentially consider your ascendant sign as a means of identifying and understanding your soul's purpose and your self-expression. Your soul's purpose will be to attain inner harmony which, in turn, will allow you naturally to co-operative with and be of service to humanity in accordance with metaphysical doctrine.

Esoteric astrology is often associated with the current age of Aquarius which transpired when the vernal equinox entered the constellation of Aquarius according to metaphysical philosophy. The Aquarian age symbolically represents the Enlightenment Era when free-thinking dominated current debate and philosophy.

EXOTERIC-ESOTERIC ASTROLOGY THERAPEUTIC TASKS

> Consider the possibility of looking into astrology for character-analysis purposes in order to enlighten yourself about your personal life and your soul's evolutionary journey.
>
> Learn the basics of exoteric astrology in order to consider your personality traits.
>
> Acquire the fundamentals of esoteric astrology in order to further your healing journey and to explore your inner mind.
>
> Consider the relationship between your sun sign and your ascendant sign from the cause-and-effect perspective.

ZODIAC SIGNS

Do you see life merely from a surface-level perspective?

Do you understand your personal strengths and weaknesses?

Can you focus on who you really are rather than who you might aspire to be?

WHAT IS A ZODIAC SIGN?

The astrological zodiac signs will consist of twelve archetypal symbols which will depict your character traits and typical reactions to circumstances according the date, time and place of your birth (see Figure 28: *Zodiac Signs*).

When considering the zodiac signs within your natal chart you should look to see which signs will have prominence generally within your chart. The most significant signs in your natal chart will be your sun sign and your ascendant sign in both exoteric and esoteric astrology. When you consider your sun sign and your ascendant sign you will be able to identity the affinity between where you are now and the way in which you might be developing during your evolutionary journey.

FIGURE 28: ZODIAC SIGNS

SIGN	SYMBOLISM
Aries	The ram
Taurus	The bull
Gemini	The twins
Cancer	The crab
Leo	The lion
Virgo	The virgin
Libra	The scales

Scorpio	The scorpion
Sagittarius	The archer
Capricorn	The goat
Aquarius	The water-carrier
Pisces	The fishes

ZODIAC SIGN NUMBERS

The astrological zodiac signs will be numbered from one to twelve (see Figure 29: *Zodiac Sign Numbers*).

Each zodiac sign will be represented by its own astrological glyph which will appear as a shorthand symbol for ease of reading in your natal chart. Each astrological glyph will depict the symbolic meaning of the zodiac sign to which it is related.

Each sign of the zodiac will be associated with a given type of symbolism which will be indicative of the iconic characteristics of the zodiac sign itself.

FIGURE 29: ZODIAC SIGN NUMBERS

NUMBER	NAME	SYMBOLISM
1	Aries	Enterprise Drive
2	Taurus	Possessions Wealth
3	Gemini	Friendship Socialising
4	Cancer	Family care Homemaking

5	Leo	Self-expression Creativity
6	Virgo	Practicality Health
7	Libra	Equality Justice
8	Scorpio	Rebirth Transformation
9	Sagittarius	Exploration Travel
10	Capricorn	Career Status
11	Aquarius	Humanity Originality
12	Pisces	Self-healing Intuition

ZODIAC SIGN ELEMENTS

Each zodiac sign will be associated with one of four archetypal elements which will exhibit certain symbolic characteristics (see Figure 30: *Zodiac Sign Elements*).

The elements of fire, earth, air and water have three of the zodiac signs in each category. The twelve signs of the zodiac are, therefore, divided into four groups of three by the zodiac sign elements.

The fire element signs will denote your desire for action and achievement. The fire signs are Aries, Leo and Sagittarius as sign numbers one, five and nine respectively.

The earth element signs will denote your desire for security and organisation. The earth signs are Taurus, Virgo and Capricorn as sign numbers two, six and ten respectively.

The air element signs will denote your desire for knowledge and information dissemination. The air signs are Gemini, Libra and Aquarius as sign numbers three, seven and eleven respectively.

The water element signs will denote your desire for emotive expression and intuitive thinking. The water signs are Cancer, Scorpio and Pisces as sign numbers four, eight and twelve respectively.

FIGURE 30: ZODIAC SIGN ELEMENTS

ELEMENT	SYMBOLISM	SIGN
Fire	Action Achievement	Aries Leo Sagittarius
Earth	Security Organisation	Taurus Virgo Capricorn
Air	Knowledge Communication	Gemini Libra Aquarius
Water	Emotive expression Intuition	Cancer Scorpio Pisces

ZODIAC SIGN QUALITIES

Each zodiac sign will be associated with one of three archetypal qualities which will exhibit certain symbolic characteristics (see Figure 31: *Zodiac Sign Qualities*).

The qualities of cardinal, fixed and mutable have four of the zodiac signs in each category. The twelve signs of the zodiac are, therefore, divided into three groups of four by the zodiac sign qualities.

The cardinal quality signs will be indicative of your desire to strive to be pioneering and enterprising. The cardinal signs are Aries, Cancer, Libra and Capricorn as sign numbers one, four, seven and ten respectively.

The fixed quality signs will be indicative of your desire to strive to be steadfast and reliable. The fixed signs are Taurus, Leo, Scorpio and Aquarius as sign numbers two, five, eight and eleven respectively.

The mutable quality signs will be indicative of your desire to strive to be adaptable and flexible. The mutable signs are Gemini, Virgo, Sagittarius and Pisces as sign numbers three, six, nine and twelve respectively.

FIGURE 31: ZODIAC SIGN QUALITIES

QUALITY	SYMBOLISM	SIGN
Cardinal	Pioneering Enterprising	Aries Cancer Libra Capricorn
Fixed	Steadfast Reliable	Taurus Leo Scorpio Aquarius
Mutable	Adaptable Flexible	Gemini Virgo Sagittarius Pisces

ZODIAC SIGN GENDERS

Each zodiac sign will be associated with one of two archetypal genders which will exhibit certain symbolic characteristics (see Figure 32: *Zodiac Sign Genders*).

The genders of masculine (or yang) and feminine (or yin) have six of the zodiac signs in each category. The twelve signs of the zodiac are, therefore, divided into two groups of six by the zodiac sign genders.

The masculine gender signs will signify your need to exhibit extrovert characteristics and to display outer strength in society. The masculine signs are the fire signs Aries, Leo and Sagittarius and the air signs Gemini, Libra and Aquarius.

The feminine gender signs will signify your need to exhibit introvert characteristics and to display inner strength in isolation. The feminine signs are the earth signs Taurus, Virgo and Capricorn and the water signs Cancer, Scorpio and Pisces.

FIGURE 32: ZODIAC SIGN GENDERS

GENDER	SYMBOLISM	SIGN
Masculine	Extrovert Outer strength	Aries Gemini Leo Libra Sagittarius Aquarius
Feminine	Introvert Inner strength	Taurus Cancer Virgo Scorpio Capricorn Pisces

ANGELIC HEALING LINKS TO ASTROLOGY

Each zodiac sign will be associated with a given archangel who will oversee your healing mission according to the nature of the specific zodiac signs in your natal chart (see Figure 33: *Angelic Healing Links to Astrology*).

The appropriate archangels will support and nurture all the attributes inherent within each zodiac sign and will enhance your healing journey accordingly.

You can consider the implications of the specific zodiac signs in your natal chart and the way in which you can be assisted by your personal archangels in the therapeutic context.

FIGURE 33: ANGELIC HEALING LINKS TO ASTROLOGY

Sign	Archangel
Aries	Ariel
Taurus	Chamuel
Gemini	Zadkiel
Cancer	Gabriel
Leo	Raziel
Virgo	Metatron
Libra	Jophiel
Scorpio	Jeremiel
Sagittarius	Raguel
Capricorn	Azrael

Aquarius	Uriel
Pisces	Sandalphon

Tarot links to astrology

Each zodiac sign will be associated with a given card from the tarot's major arcana which will enhance your understanding of astrological symbolism and the attributes of your psyche (see Figure 34: *Tarot Links to Astrology*).

You can consider the implications of the specific zodiac signs in your natal chart and the way in which you can relate to tarot imagery and symbolism in the therapeutic context.

FIGURE 34: TAROT LINKS TO ASTROLOGY

SIGN	TAROT CARD
Aries	The emperor
Taurus	The hierophant
Gemini	The lovers
Cancer	The chariot
Leo	Strength
Virgo	The hermit
Libra	Justice
Scorpio	Death

Sagittarius	Temperance
Capricorn	The devil
Aquarius	The star
Pisces	The moon

ZODIAC SIGNS THERAPEUTIC TASKS

Consider each zodiac sign in terms of its sign element, quality and gender in order to obtain a basic picture of the attributes and motivations of humankind.

Reflect on the nature of your sun sign and your ascendant sign in terms of the inherent symbolic attributes of these signs as applicable to you.

Undertake some meditative practice in order to contemplate the significance of your sun sign and your ascendant sign for your life and your healing journey.

Undertake some meditative practice in order to contact the archangel associated with your sun sign and your ascendant sign and invoke the assistance of these light beings.

Undertake some meditative practice in order to highlight the significance of the card from the tarot's major arcana which will be associated with your sun sign and your ascendant sign.

PLANETARY SIGNS

Can you appreciate that external influences in your life cannot be ignored?

Could you make the most of your personal attributes and accomplishments within the social world?

Would you be able to explore your hidden talents and to congratulate yourself on your achievements?

WHAT IS A PLANETARY SIGN?

Planetary signs will denote those external influences which you will encounter when you travel through life in an effort to survive in the social world (see Figure 35: *Planetary Signs*).

You should note the position of all the planets in your natal chart and observe which zodiac signs each had been transiting at the time of your birth in order to see the way in which your zodiac signs are expressed.

Each planetary sign has its own astrological glyph for ease of reading in your natal chart.

FIGURE 35: PLANETARY SIGNS

PLANET	SYMBOLISM
Sun	Self-expression Creativity
Moon	Emotive expression Intuition
Mercury	Intellect Communication
Mars	Enterprise Drive
Venus	Love Creative arts

Jupiter	Experience Potential
Saturn	Status Vocation
Neptune	Healing Nurturing
Uranus	Originality Humanity
Pluto	Transformation Liberation
Earth	Practicality Methodology
Vulcan	Realisation Enlightenment

INNER PLANETS

The five inner planets will symbolically represent your day-to-day experiences and the effect which these events can have on your existence (see Figure 36: *Inner Planets*).

The inner planets will comprise Sun, Moon, Mercury, Mars and Venus. All the inner planets will feature in both exoteric and esoteric astrology.

FIGURE 36: INNER PLANETS

SUN	MOON	MERCURY	MARS	VENUS

OUTER PLANETS

The five outer planets will symbolically represent your lifetime's experiences and the way in which major events can shape your existence (see Figure 37: *Outer Planets*).

The outer planets will comprise Jupiter, Saturn, Neptune, Uranus and Pluto. All the outer planets will feature in both exoteric and esoteric astrology.

FIGURE 37: OUTER PLANETS

| JUPITER | SATURN | NEPTUNE | URANUS | PLUTO |

EXOTERIC-ESOTERIC PLANETS

The twelve zodiac signs will be closely associated with the planetary signs according to both exoteric and esoteric astrology (see Figure 38: *Exoteric-Esoteric Planets*).

The ten planets used within exoteric astrology will comprise Sun, Moon, Mercury, Mars and Venus as the five inner planets and Jupiter, Saturn, Neptune, Uranus and Pluto as the five outer planets. Within exoteric astrology, consequently, Mercury and Venus will both be associated with two zodiac signs.

The twelve planets used within esoteric astrology will comprise Sun, Moon, Mercury, Mars and Venus as the five inner planets and Jupiter, Saturn, Neptune, Uranus and Pluto as the five outer planets and, in addition, Earth and Vulcan. Within esoteric astrology, consequently, each zodiac sign will have a separate planetary sign with which it will be associated.

FIGURE 38: EXOTERIC-ESOTERIC PLANETS

SIGN	EXOTERIC PLANET	ESOTERIC PLANET
Aries	Mars	Mercury
Taurus	Venus	Vulcan
Gemini	Mercury	Venus

Cancer	Moon	Neptune
Leo	Sun	Sun
Virgo	Mercury	Moon
Libra	Venus	Uranus
Scorpio	Pluto	Mars
Sagittarius	Jupiter	Earth
Capricorn	Saturn	Saturn
Aquarius	Uranus	Jupiter
Pisces	Neptune	Pluto

PLANETARY SIGNS THERAPEUTIC TASKS

Reflect on the influence of the inner planets and the outer planets in your natal chart.

Contemplate the nature of your principal planetary signs and the zodiac signs in which each resides in your natal chart.

Consider the influence on you of both your exoteric planets and your esoteric planets and the symbolism which will be associated with each planet in your natal chart.

Undertake some meditative practice in order to contemplate the significance of your planetary sign investigation for your life and your healing journey.

ASTROLOGICAL HOUSES

Can you attain a balance between what you desire and what you already possess?

Could you focus on your creative talents for a life-affirming and pleasurable project?

Do you see yourself as a constantly evolving being?

WHAT IS AN ASTROLOGICAL HOUSE?

The astrological houses will consider the spheres of activity and the experience which you might encounter in your everyday existence.

The zodiac signs which were being transited by a given planetary sign in your natal chart will each reside in one of twelve different astrological houses. You will need, consequently, to consider each entry in your natal chart in terms of the planetary signs which transit your zodiac signs and the astrological houses in which each resides as a threefold dimension of your unique interpretation.

ASTROLOGICAL HOUSE NUMBERS

Each of the twelve astrological houses will be numbered in order to correspond with its associated zodiac sign and will embody its own symbolism (see Figure 39: *Astrological Houses*).

FIGURE 39: ASTROLOGICAL HOUSES

House	Symbolism	Sign
First	Self-awareness and identity Conscious mind and physicality Personality and soul	Aries
Second	Values and possessions Resources and finances Gifts and security	Taurus

Third	Intellect and communication Information dissemination Siblings and friends	Gemini
Fourth	Home and family Motherhood and mother-figures Safety and nurturing	Cancer
Fifth	Self-expression and creativity Love and generosity Children and minors	Leo
Sixth	Work and health Service and healing Order and method	Virgo
Seventh	Relationships and partnerships Law and order Stability and balance	Libra
Eight	Rebirth and transformation Death and afterlife Sexuality and sexual-identity	Scorpio
Ninth	Philosophy and education Travel and exploration Aspirations and goals	Sagittarius
Tenth	Status and profession Responsibilities and duties Fatherhood and father-figures	Capricorn
Eleventh	Humanity and compassion Friendships and communities Innovation and originality	Aquarius

| Twelve | Emotive expression and intuition
Unconscious mind and dreams
Mysticism and psychic phenomenon | Pisces |

ASTROLOGICAL HOUSE MODES

Each house will be associated with a specific house mode which will correspond to the qualities of the zodiac signs (see Figure 40: *Astrological House Modes*).

The angular house modes will be related to the cardinal quality zodiac signs which will embody pioneering and enterprising factors. The angular house modes will, therefore, be closely associated with the zodiac signs Aries, Cancer, Libra and Capricorn as astrological house numbers one, four, seven and ten respectively.

The succedent house modes will be related to the fixed quality zodiac signs which will embody steadfast and reliable factors. The succedent house modes will, therefore, be closely associated with the zodiac signs Taurus, Leo, Scorpio and Aquarius as astrological house numbers two, five, eight and eleven respectively.

The cadent house modes will be related to the mutable quality zodiac signs which will embody adaptable and flexible factors. The cadent house modes will, therefore, be closely associated with the zodiac signs Gemini, Virgo, Sagittarius and Pisces as astrological house numbers three, six, nine and twelve respectively.

You should consider the astrological house modes which are represented in your natal chart in order to gauge your character traits and your natural inclinations in the therapeutic context.

FIGURE 40: ASTROLOGICAL HOUSE MODES

MODE	SYMBOLISM	SIGN
Angular	Pioneering Enterprising	Aries Cancer Libra Capricorn
Succedent	Steadfast Reliable	Taurus Leo Scorpio Aquarius
Cadent	Adaptable Flexible	Gemini Virgo Sagittarius Pisces

ASTROLOGICAL HOUSES THERAPEUTIC TASKS

Consider the nature of the astrological houses in which your zodiac signs and your planetary signs reside in your natal chart.

Reflect on the symbolism associated with each astrological house which is represented in your natal chart.

Contemplate the house modes which are represented in your natal chart and the zodiac signs with which each is associated.

Undertake some meditative practice in order to discover the significance of your astrological house mode investigation for your life and your healing journey.

SIGN-PLANET-HOUSE CONFIGURATION

Can you look at yourself deeply in the context of your existence?

Could you take an overview of your life's purpose?

Do you appreciate that you are a multi-faceted entity in your own right?

WHAT IS A SIGN-PLANET-HOUSE CONFIGURATION?

Your astrological natal chart will comprise a set of entries for every planet which will be transiting a given zodiac sign and will be residing within a single astrological house. This unique configuration at the date, time and place of your birth will be the snapshot which will define you as an individual in astrological terms.

You should consider each sign-planet-house configuration in your natal chart in order to fully assess the astrological influence on you and your life. You should, of course, bear in mind that every planet will be represented in your natal chart but not every zodiac sign or every astrological house.

ARIES-FIRST HOUSE

The zodiac sign of Aries, the ram, as a fire element will symbolise the characteristics of a desire for action and achievement coupled with the cardinal qualities of being pioneering and enterprising and the extrovert masculine gender (see Figure 41: *Aries*).

Aries will be related to the planet Mars in exoteric astrology and the planet Mercury in esoteric astrology. This transition will signify that Aries will be moving from a purely physical approach to existence to a more intellectual concept of survival and enterprise.

If Aries is strong in your natal chart your soul purpose in esoteric astrology will, consequently, be principally to inspire others with your inspirational ideas and your motivational drive.

FIGURE 41: ARIES

Element	Quality	Gender	House	Exoteric Planet	Esoteric Planet
Fire	Cardinal	Masculine	First	Mars	Mercury

TAURUS-SECOND HOUSE

The zodiac sign of Taurus, the bull, as an earth element will symbolise the characteristics of a desire for security and organisation coupled with the fixed quality of being steadfast and reliable and the introvert feminine gender (see Figure 42: *Taurus*).

Taurus will be related to the planet Venus in exoteric astrology and the planet Vulcan in esoteric astrology. This transition will signify that Taurus will be moving from a solely romantic approach to existence to a more grounded concept of security and wealth accumulation.

If Taurus is strong in your natal chart your soul purpose in esoteric astrology will, consequently, be principally to create a safe and grounded existence for yourself and others.

FIGURE 42: TAURUS

Element	Quality	Gender	House	Exoteric Planet	Esoteric Planet
Earth	Fixed	Feminine	Second	Venus	Vulcan

GEMINI-THIRD HOUSE

The zodiac sign of Gemini, the twins, as an air element will symbolise the characteristics of a desire for knowledge and communication coupled with the mutable qualities of being adaptable and flexible and the extrovert masculine gender (see Figure 43: *Gemini*).

Gemini will be related to the planet Mercury in exoteric astrology and the planet Venus in esoteric astrology. This transition will signify that

Gemini will be moving from a solely intellectual approach to existence to a more creative concept of communication and information acquisition.

If Gemini is strong in your natal chart your soul purpose in esoteric astrology will, consequently, be principally to acquire knowledge for yourself and to imaginatively disseminate information for the good of humanity.

FIGURE 43: GEMINI

ELEMENT	QUALITY	GENDER	HOUSE	EXOTERIC PLANET	ESOTERIC PLANET
Air	Mutable	Masculine	Third	Mercury	Venus

CANCER-FOURTH HOUSE

The zodiac sign of Cancer, the crab, as a water element will symbolise the characteristics of a desire for emotive expression and intuition coupled with the cardinal qualities of being pioneering and enterprising and the introvert feminine gender (see Figure 44: *Cancer*).

Cancer will be related to the planet Moon in exoteric astrology and the planet Neptune in esoteric astrology. This transition will signify that Cancer will be moving from a solely functional approach to existence to a more developmental concept of caring for home and family.

If Cancer is strong in your natal chart your soul purpose in esoteric astrology will, consequently, be principally to build a spiritual and nurturing home environment for yourself and your family.

FIGURE 44: CANCER

ELEMENT	QUALITY	GENDER	HOUSE	EXOTERIC PLANET	ESOTERIC PLANET
Water	Cardinal	Feminine	Fourth	Moon	Neptune

LEO-FIFTH HOUSE

The zodiac sign of Leo, the lion, as a fire element will symbolise the characteristics of a desire for action and achievement coupled with the fixed qualities of being steadfast and reliable and the extrovert masculine gender (see Figure 45: *Leo*).

Leo will be related to the planet Sun in both exoteric astrology and esoteric astrology. This status quo situation will signify that Leo will be moving from a solely self-interested approach to existence to a more humanitarian concept of self-expression and interaction with others.

If Leo is strong in your natal chart your soul purpose in esoteric astrology will, consequently, be principally to express qualities of generosity, creativity and leadership.

FIGURE 45: LEO

ELEMENT	QUALITY	GENDER	HOUSE	EXOTERIC PLANET	ESOTERIC PLANET
Fire	Fixed	Masculine	Fifth	Sun	Sun

VIRGO-SIXTH HOUSE

The zodiac sign of Virgo, the virgin, as an earth element will symbolise the characteristics of a desire for security and organisation coupled with the mutable qualities of being adaptable and flexible and the introvert feminine gender (see Figure 46: *Virgo*).

Virgo will be related to the planet Mercury in exoteric astrology and the planet Moon in esoteric astrology. This transition will signify that Virgo will be moving from a solely intellectual approach to existence to a more self-caring concept of service to mankind.

If Virgo is strong in your natal chart your soul purpose in esoteric astrology will, consequently, be principally to heal and serve others without sacrificing yourself.

FIGURE 46: VIRGO

ELEMENT	QUALITY	GENDER	HOUSE	EXOTERIC PLANET	ESOTERIC PLANET
Earth	Mutable	Feminine	Sixth	Mercury	Moon

LIBRA-SEVENTH HOUSE

The zodiac sign of Libra, the scales, as an air element will symbolise the characteristics of a desire for knowledge and communication coupled with the cardinal qualities of being pioneering and enterprising and the extrovert masculine gender (see Figure 47: *Libra*).

Libra will be related to the planet Venus in exoteric astrology and the planet Uranus in esoteric astrology. This transition will signify that Libra will be moving from a solely idealistic approach to existence to a more humanitarian concept of justice and equality.

If Libra is strong in your natal chart your soul purpose in esoteric astrology will, consequently, be principally to strive for harmony and equality for yourself and humankind.

FIGURE 47: LIBRA

ELEMENT	QUALITY	GENDER	HOUSE	EXOTERIC PLANET	ESOTERIC PLANET
Air	Cardinal	Masculine	Seventh	Venus	Uranus

SCORPIO-EIGHTH HOUSE

The zodiac sign of Scorpio, the scorpion, as a water element will symbolise the characteristics of a desire for emotive expression and intuition coupled with the fixed qualities of being steadfast and reliable and the introvert feminine gender (see Figure 48: *Scorpio*).

Scorpio will be related to the planet Pluto in exoteric astrology and the planet Mars in esoteric astrology. This transition will signify that Scorpio will be moving from a solely liberating approach to existence to a more focused concept of rebirthing and personal transformation.

If Scorpio is strong in your natal chart your soul purpose in esoteric astrology will, consequently, be principally to resolve the conflict within your inner soul and your outer personality.

FIGURE 48: SCORPIO

ELEMENT	QUALITY	GENDER	HOUSE	EXOTERIC PLANET	ESOTERIC PLANET
Water	Fixed	Feminine	Eighth	Pluto	Mars

SAGITTARIUS-NINTH HOUSE

The zodiac sign of Sagittarius, the archer, as a fire element will symbolise the characteristics of a desire for action and achievement coupled with the mutable qualities of being adaptable and flexible and the extrovert masculine gender (see Figure 49: *Sagittarius*).

Sagittarius will be related to the planet Jupiter in exoteric astrology and the planet Earth in esoteric astrology. This transition will signify that Sagittarius will be moving from a solely hedonistic approach to existence to a more philosophical concept of exploration and mind-broadening.

If Sagittarius is strong in your natal chart your soul purpose in esoteric astrology will, consequently, be principally to uphold your personal truth and inner wisdom as an example to others.

FIGURE 49: SAGITTARIUS

ELEMENT	QUALITY	GENDER	HOUSE	EXOTERIC PLANET	ESOTERIC PLANET
Fire	Mutable	Masculine	Ninth	Jupiter	Earth

CAPRICORN-TENTH HOUSE

The zodiac sign of Capricorn, the goat, as an earth element will symbolise the characteristics of a desire for security and organisation coupled with the cardinal qualities of being pioneering and enterprising and the introvert feminine gender (see Figure 50: *Capricorn*).

Capricorn will be related to the planet Saturn in both exoteric astrology and esoteric astrology. This status quo situation will signify that Capricorn will be moving from a solely self-centred approach to vocation to a more spiritual concept of status and career-advancement.

If Capricorn is strong in your natal chart your soul purpose in esoteric astrology will, consequently, be principally to adopt a spiritual vocation and purpose for the greater good.

FIGURE 50: CAPRICORN

ELEMENT	QUALITY	GENDER	HOUSE	EXOTERIC PLANET	ESOTERIC PLANET
Earth	Cardinal	Feminine	Tenth	Saturn	Saturn

AQUARIUS-ELEVENTH HOUSE

The zodiac sign of Aquarius, the water-carrier, as an air element will symbolise the characteristics of a desire for knowledge and communication coupled with the fixed qualities of being steadfast and reliable and the extrovert masculine gender (see Figure 51: *Aquarius*).

Aquarius will be related to the planet Uranus in exoteric astrology and the planet Jupiter in esoteric astrology. This transition will signify that Aquarius will be moving from a solely group-welfare approach to existence to a more philosophical concept of humanitarianism and original thinking.

If Aquarius is strong in your natal chart your soul purpose in esoteric astrology will, consequently, be principally to creatively serve and enlighten humanity by example.

FIGURE 51: AQUARIUS

ELEMENT	QUALITY	GENDER	HOUSE	EXOTERIC PLANET	ESOTERIC PLANET
Air	Fixed	Masculine	Eleventh	Uranus	Jupiter

PISCES-TWELFTH HOUSE

The zodiac sign of Pisces, the fishes, as a water element will symbolise the characteristics of a desire for emotive expression and intuition coupled with the mutable qualities of being adaptable and flexible and the introvert feminine gender (see Figure 52: *Pisces*).

Pisces will be related to the planet Neptune in exoteric astrology and the planet Pluto in esoteric astrology. This transition will signify that Pisces will be moving from a solely dreamlike approach to existence to a more go-getting concept of self-healing and intuition.

If Pisces is strong in your natal chart your soul purpose in esoteric astrology will, consequently, be principally to heal and nurture yourself and others.

FIGURE 52: PISCES

ELEMENT	QUALITY	GENDER	HOUSE	EXOTERIC PLANET	ESOTERIC PLANET
Water	Mutable	Feminine	Twelfth	Neptune	Pluto

SIGN-PLANET-HOUSE CONFIGURATION THERAPEUTIC TASKS

> Consider the nature of each entry in your natal chart in terms of the threefold relationship between each sign, planet and house configuration.

> Reflect on the way in which each sign-planet-house feature will interact and interweave into your existence in order to analyse your character as a holistic and organic entity.
>
> Undertake some meditative practice in order to contemplate the significance of your unique sign-planet-house configuration investigation for your life and your healing journey.

ASTROLOGICAL AXES

Can you see the inherent conflicts within your mind?

Are you aware of the polarity factors which govern your existence?

Do you appreciate that you have an inner world and an outer social sphere?

WHAT IS AN ASTROLOGICAL AXIS?

Astrological axes will highlight counter-balances and complementary factors within your psyche which will act as personality stabilisers and will provide you with perspective on your life. You can understand and interpret your natal chart more accurately if you are aware of the inherent polar opposites within astrology in general and the significance for you in particular.

The therapeutic significance of natal chart axes originated principally with Jungian theories about polarity principles whereby your mind will harbour opposing factors, conflicting responses and complementary elements simultaneously.

OPPOSING ZODIAC SIGNS

The opposing zodiac signs are those signs which are polar opposites in terms of their position within the zodiac (see Figure 53: *Opposing Zodiac Signs*).

These pairs of signs will allow you to discover the way in which your psyche and your life can develop by taking the essence from the opposite sign number as a stabilising factor. Every zodiac sign will, consequently, possess the characteristics of the opposing sign contained within it and this knowledge will serve as a counter-balance for you.

The first set of six zodiac signs from Aries to Virgo will embody an internal focus and will denote the way in which your life might unfold.

The second set of six zodiac signs from Libra to Pisces will be more externally directed towards your social world and the way in which you can interact with others.

FIGURE 53: OPPOSING ZODIAC SIGNS

INNER SYMBOLISM	OPPOSING SIGNS	OUTER SYMBOLISM
Self-awareness	Aries – Libra	Universal awareness
Material acquisition	Taurus – Scorpio	Spiritual acquisition
Personal learning	Gemini – Sagittarius	Universal learning
Home-orientation	Cancer – Capricorn	Career-orientation
Self-love	Leo – Aquarius	Universal love
Universal healing	Virgo – Pisces	Self-healing

ASCENDANT AND DESCENDANT AXIS

The two most important opposing zodiac signs in your natal chart will be your ascendant sign and your descendant sign (see Figure 54: *AC-DC Axis*).

The ascendant sign in your natal chart will denote where the sun was rising on the eastern horizontal at the moment of your birth.

Your ascendant sign (AC) will signify that part of your psyche which you will display to the outside world as your social mask (or social persona). Your ascendant sign will allow you to interact and to adapt to your social surroundings in order to survive as part of the herd and, therefore, will govern your social relationships.

Your ascendant sign will always be located on the cusp of the first house in your natal chart. Your ascendant sign in esoteric astrology will depict the path of your healing mission according to this sign's specific characteristics.

The descendant sign in your natal chart will denote where the sun was setting on the western horizontal at the moment of your birth.

Your descendant sign (DC) will signify the face which you do not show to the world at large as this aspect of your psyche will contain your inner thoughts, feelings and responses to life and circumstances as your personal persona (or shadow self). Your descendant sign will empower you to tap into your innermost thoughts and feelings in order to gain self-knowledge and awareness and, therefore, will govern your intimate relationships.

Your descendant sign will always be located on the cusp of the seventh house in your natal chart. Your descendant sign in esoteric astrology will depict the key to your healing mission according to this sign's specific characteristics.

Your AC-DC axis will show you the way in which your public and private identity will interweave in order to create a rounded picture of your psyche, your motivations and the true essence to your healing journey.

FIGURE 54: AC-DC AXIS

ASCENDANT SIGN	DESCENDANT SIGN
Social persona	Personal persona
Social relationships	Intimate relationships
First house cusp	Seventh house cusp

IMUM COELI AND MEDIUM COELI AXIS

The imum coeli and medium coeli axis in your natal chart will represent your spiritual development and your confidence in the social world (see Figure 55: *IC-MC Axis*).

The imum coeli (IC) will symbolise your origins in infancy as the place where your life path began. Your imum coeli will be located at the lowest point (or nadir) of your natal chart and will always be located on the cusp of the fourth house.

The medium coeli (MC) will symbolise your maturity as the place where your life path will be heading. Your medium coeli will be located at the highest point (or zenith) of your natal chart and will always be located on the cusp of the tenth house.

Your IC-MC axis will allow you to see the way in which your psyche has developed from the past and the way in which you can develop spiritually in the future.

FIGURE 55: IC-MC AXIS

IMUM COELI	MEDIUM COELI
Path from infancy	Path to maturity
Lowest chart point	Highest chart point
Fourth house cusp	Tenth house cusp

SOUTH NODE AND NORTH NODE AXIS

The south node (or descending node) and the north node (or ascending node) are lunar nodes in your natal chart which will depict your healing journey through life (see Figure 56: *South Node-North Node Axis*).

The south node will denote the causes of your karmic history according to its position in your natal chart. Your south node will, consequently, indicate those character traits and personal inclinations which might be unrealised or undeveloped within your psyche.

The north node will denote the effects of your karmic history according to its position in your natal chart. The position of your north node will, consequently, indicate those character traits and personal indications which might be realised or developed within your psyche.

The north node-south node axis, therefore, will denote your karmic journey and your personal psychic evolution.

FIGURE 56: SOUTH NODE-NORTH NODE AXIS

SOUTH NODE	NORTH NODE
Karmic cause Unrealised character traits	Karmic effect Realised character traits

HEMISPHERES

You can divide your natal chart into four hemispheres which will denote the directions of north, south, west and east in order to symbolically gauge your healing mission and your character inclinations (see Figure 57: *Natal Chart Hemispheres*).

The division of your natal chart into hemispheres will be dictated by the position of your AC-DC axis and your IC-MC axis.

The northern hemisphere of your natal chart will symbolise your introvert traits and your subjective thinking and will be associated with your higher chakra system. The northern hemisphere of your natal chart will comprise the house numbers seven to twelve.

The southern hemisphere of your natal chart will symbolise your extrovert traits and your objective thinking and will be associated with your lower chakra system. The southern hemisphere of your natal chart will comprise the house numbers one to six.

The western hemisphere of your natal chart will symbolise your inner personal motivation and will be associated with your lower chakra system. The western hemisphere in your natal chart will comprise the house numbers three to ten.

The eastern hemisphere of your natal chart will symbolise your outer social motivation and will be associated with your higher chakra system. The eastern hemisphere of your natal chart will comprise the house numbers four to nine.

You should note the strengths of the hemispheres in your natal chart in order to gain an understanding of your personal inclinations or disinclinations and the way in which these tendencies will affect your healing journey.

FIGURE 57: NATAL CHART HEMISPHERES

HEMISPHERE	CHAKRA SYSTEM	SYMBOLISM	HOUSES
Northern	Higher	Introvert Subjective thinking	7 – 12
Southern	Lower	Extrovert Objective thinking	1 – 6
Western	Lower	Inner motivation	3 – 10
Eastern	Higher	Outer motivation	4 – 9

QUADRANTS

You can divide your natal chart into four quadrants in order to gauge your personal tendencies and your social inclinations (see Figure 58: *Natal Chart Quadrants*).

The division of your natal chart into quadrants will be dictated by the position of your AC-DC axis and your IC-MC axis.

The first quadrant of your natal chart will symbolise your personal identity. The first quadrant of your natal chart will comprise the house numbers one to three.

The second quadrant of your natal chart will symbolise your self-expression. The second quadrant of your natal chart will comprise the house numbers four to six.

The third quadrant of your natal chart will symbolise your social identity. The third quadrant of your natal chart will comprise the house numbers seven to nine.

The fourth quadrant of your natal chart will symbolise your social expression. The fourth quadrant of your natal chart will comprise the house numbers ten to twelve.

You should note the strengths of the quadrants in your natal chart in order to gain an understanding of your character traits and your social inclinations and the way in which these tendencies will affect your healing journey.

FIGURE 58: NATAL CHART QUADRANTS

QUADRANT	SYMBOLISM	HOUSES
First	Personal identity	1- 3
Second	Self-expression	4 – 6
Third	Social identity	7 – 9
Fourth	Social expression	10 – 12

ASTROLOGICAL AXES THERAPEUTIC TASKS

Consider the nature of the opposing zodiac signs in your natal chart.

Reflect on the nature of the AC-DC axis zodiac signs in your natal chart in order to appreciate the significance of your inner and your outer worlds.

Contemplate the nature of the IC-MC axis zodiac signs in your natal chart in order to appreciate the significance of your life path.

Ponder the nature of the north node-south node axis zodiac signs in your natal chart in order to appreciate the significance of your therapeutic journey.

Assess the significance and strengths of your natal chart hemispheres and quadrants in order to gauge your relationship with yourself and others in the social world.

> Undertake some meditative practice in order to contemplate the significance of your astrological axes investigation for your life and your healing journey.

NATAL CHART

Could you examine yourself from a number of different angles?

Are you able to accept yourself for who you really are?

Can you recognise the conflicting factors which your psyche embodies?

WHAT IS A NATAL CHART?

Your natal chart will be designed to show the twelve houses with the planetary signs and the zodiac signs within these houses using a divided circle format (see Figure 59: *Natal Chart*).

You will need to obtain some form of natal chart which you can study in order to be able to interpret the symbolic value of the planetary signs which reside in specific zodiac signs and astrological houses. You will be able to construct your natal chart using astrological software which will normally be freely available on the internet. You will require the date, time and place of your birth in order to construct your natal chart.

There are twelve astrological houses in both esoteric and exoteric astrology. These astrological houses will sit in fixed positions within your natal chart although each house may not appear as identical in size depending on the way in which your natal chart has been constructed. Normally the first house will sit on the extreme left of your natal chart in order to indicate the position of your ascendant sign.

The planetary signs transiting the zodiac signs will be indicated by glyphs in your natal chart. Each planet will only appear once since its position will be fixed at the moment of your birth although one zodiac sign can have several planetary signs which are transiting that sign simultaneously. Your natal chart will show the astrological axes which will apply to you either indicated by arrows for the AC-DC and the IC-MC axes or by glyphs for the south node-north node axis.

You may also wish to consult a competent astrologer who will be fully conversant with exoteric and esoteric astrology in order to give yourself a more personal in-depth reading. This book will provide you with only a cursory overview of astrology as an essential starting-point for your therapeutic investigation.

FIGURE 59: NATAL CHART

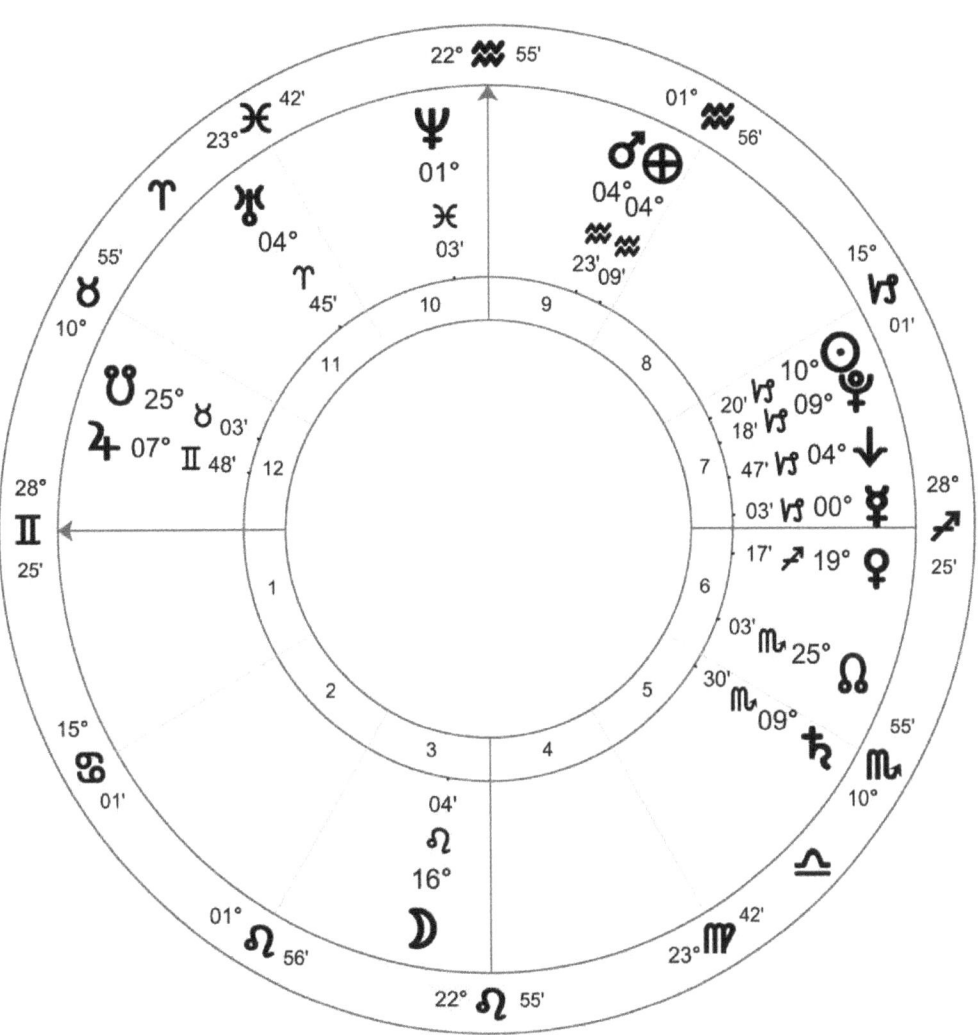

NATAL CHART INTERPRETATION

You will need to read and interpret each entry in your natal chart in terms of the planet transiting a given zodiac sign and the astrological house in which it resides in order to decipher zodiac sign characteristics, planetary sign influences and house life spheres which will be reflected in each of your sign-planet-house configurations (see Figure 60: *Natal Chart Configurations*).

This form of threefold sign-planet-house configuration reading will then form the basis of your astrological interpretation.

Always look initially to see what might appear as a strength in your natal chart in terms of your sun sign. The most prominent strength in the natal chart example would be Capricorn as the sun sign in the seventh house. Capricorn is also generally prominent in the seventh astrological house of relationships and partnerships.

Further strengths will be found in the astrological axes, hemispheres and quadrants of your natal chart.

FIGURE 60: NATAL CHART CONFIGURATIONS

PLANET	SIGN	HOUSE
Sun	Capricorn ♑	Seventh
Moon	Leo ♌	Third
Mercury	Capricorn ♑	Seventh
Mars	Aquarius ♒	Ninth
Venus	Sagittarius ♐	Sixth
Jupiter	Gemini ♊	Twelfth
Saturn	Scorpio ♏	Fifth
Neptune	Pisces ♓	Tenth
Uranus	Aries ♈	Eleventh

Pluto	Capricorn ♑	Seventh
Earth	Aquarius ♒	Ninth
Vulcan	Capricorn ♑	Seventh

NATAL CHART AXES

You should consider the astrological axes in your natal chart as an enhancement to your self-knowledge with astrology (see Figure 61: *Natal Chart Axes*).

Always look to see what might appear as a strength in your natal chart in terms of your AC-DC axis, your IC-MC axis and your south node-north node axis.

The ascendant-descendant axis in the natal chart example has been shown as an arrow passing from the far right-hand aspect of the chart as the DC sign to the far left-hand aspect of the chart as the AC sign. The AC resides in Gemini while the DC sits in Sagittarius as the greatest axis prominence within this chart.

The imum coeli-medium coeli axis in the natal chart example has been shown as an arrow passing from the nadir at bottom of the chart as the IC to the zenith at the top of the chart as the MC. The IC resides in Leo while the MC sits in Aquarius as the life path indications within this natal chart.

The south node-north node axis in the natal chart example has been indicated by the ascending node and the descending node glyphs for the lunar nodes. The south node resides in Taurus in the twelfth house while the north node sits in Scorpio in the sixth house as the healing journey indications within this natal chart.

FIGURE 61: NATAL CHART AXES

AXIS	SIGN	HOUSE
Ascendant sign	Gemini ♊	First cusp

Descendant sign	Sagittarius ♐	Seventh cusp
Imum coeli	Leo ♌	Fourth cusp
Medium coeli	Aquarius ♒	Tenth cusp
South node	Taurus ♉	Twelfth
North node	Scorpio ♏	Sixth

NATAL CHART SIGN ELEMENTS

You should consider the balance within your natal chart in terms of zodiac sign elements as an enhancement to your self-knowledge with astrology (see Figure 62: *Natal Chart Sign Elements*).

The configuration of zodiac sign elements in the natal chart example shows an emphasis on the fire element, the earth element and the air element with less weight on the water element when considering both the zodiac signs and the chart axes.

The fire sign element has been represented in the zodiac signs Aries, Leo and Sagittarius together with the DC in Sagittarius and the IC in Leo.

The earth sign element has been represented in the zodiac sign Capricorn together with the south node in Taurus.

The air sign element has been represented in the zodiac signs Gemini and Aquarius together with the AC in Gemini and the MC in Aquarius.

The water sign element has been represented in the zodiac signs Scorpio and Pisces together with the north node in Scorpio.

FIGURE 62: NATAL CHART SIGN ELEMENTS

ELEMENT	SIGN	AXIS	STRENGTHS
Fire	Aries x 1 Leo x 1 Sagittarius x 1	Leo IC Sagittarius DC	5

Earth	Capricorn × 4	Taurus	5
Air	Gemini × 1 Aquarius × 2	Gemini AC Aquarius MC	5
Water	Scorpio × 1 Pisces × 1	Scorpio	3

NATAL CHART SIGN QUALITIES

You should consider the balance within your natal chart in terms of zodiac sign qualities as an enhancement to your self-knowledge with astrology (see Figure 63: *Natal Chart Sign Qualities*).

The configuration of zodiac sign qualities in the natal chart example shows an emphasis on the fixed quality with less weight on the cardinal quality and the mutable quality when considering both the zodiac signs and the chart axes.

The cardinal sign quality has been represented in the zodiac signs Aries and Capricorn.

The fixed sign quality has been represented in the zodiac signs Scorpio, Leo and Aquarius together with Leo and Aquarius in the IC-MC axis and Taurus and Scorpio in the south node-north node axis.

The mutable sign quality has been represented in the zodiac signs Gemini, Sagittarius and Pisces together with Gemini and Sagittarius in the AC-DC axis.

FIGURE 63: NATAL CHART SIGN QUALITIES

QUALITY	SIGN	AXIS	STRENGTHS
Cardinal	Aries × 1 Capricorn × 4		5

		Leo IC	
Fixed	Scorpio x 1 Leo x 1 Aquarius x 2	Aquarius MC Taurus Scorpio	8
Mutable	Gemini x 1 Sagittarius x 1 Pisces x 1	Gemini AC Sagittarius DC	5

NATAL CHART SIGN GENDERS

You should consider the balance within your natal chart in terms of zodiac sign genders as an enhancement to your self-knowledge with astrology (see Figure 64: *Natal Chart Sign Genders*).

The configuration of zodiac sign genders in the natal chart example shows an emphasis on the feminine gender with less weight on the masculine gender when considering both the zodiac signs and the chart axes.

The masculine gender has been represented in the zodiac signs Aries, Gemini, Leo, Sagittarius and Aquarius together with Leo and Aquarius in the IC-MC axis.

The feminine gender has been represented in the zodiac signs Scorpio, Capricorn and Pisces together with Gemini and Sagittarius in the AC-DC axis and Taurus and Scorpio in the south node-north node axis.

FIGURE 64: NATAL CHART SIGN GENDERS

GENDER	SIGN	AXIS	STRENGTHS
Masculine	Aries x 1 Gemini x 1 Leo x 1 Sagittarius x 1 Aquarius x 2	Leo IC Aquarius MC	8

Feminine	Scorpio x 1 Capricorn x 4 Pisces x 1	Taurus Gemini AC Scorpio Sagittarius DC	10

NATAL CHART HOUSE MODES

You should consider the balance within your natal chart in terms of astrological house modes as an enhancement to your self-knowledge with astrology (see Figure 65: *Natal Chart House Modes*).

The configuration of astrological house modes in the natal chart example shows an emphasis on the cadent house mode with less weight on the angular house mode and the succedent house mode when considering both the zodiac signs and the chart axes.

The angular house mode has been represented by the zodiac signs Capricorn in the seventh house and Pisces in the tenth house.

The succedent house mode has been represented by the zodiac signs Scorpio in the fifth house and Aries in the eleventh house.

The cadent house mode has been represented by the zodiac signs Leo in the third house, Sagittarius and the north node in Scorpio in the sixth house, Aquarius in the ninth house and Gemini and the south node in Taurus in the twelfth house.

FIGURE 65: NATAL CHART HOUSE MODES

MODE	HOUSE	SIGN	AXIS	STRENGTHS
Angular	Seventh	Capricorn x 4		5
	Tenth	Pisces x 1		
Succedent	Fifth	Scorpio x 1		2
	Eleventh	Aries x 1		
Cadent	Third	Leo x 1		7

	Sixth	Sagittarius x 1	Scorpio	
	Ninth	Aquarius x 2		
	Twelfth	Gemini x 1	Taurus	

NATAL CHART HEMISPHERES

You should consider the balance within your natal chart in terms of astrological hemispheres as an enhancement to your self-knowledge with astrology (see Figure 66: *Natal Chart Hemispheres*).

The configuration of hemispheres in the natal chart example shows an emphasis on the northern hemisphere and the eastern hemisphere with less weight on the southern hemisphere and the western hemisphere when considering both the zodiac signs and the chart axes.

The northern hemisphere has been represented by the zodiac signs Aries, Gemini, Capricorn, Aquarius and Pisces together with the south node in Taurus.

The southern hemisphere has been represented by the zodiac signs Leo, Scorpio and Sagittarius together with the north node in Scorpio.

The western hemisphere has been represented by the zodiac signs Aries, Gemini, Leo and Pisces together with the south node in Taurus.

The eastern hemisphere has been represented by the zodiac signs Scorpio, Sagittarius, Capricorn and Aquarius together with the north node in Scorpio.

FIGURE 66: NATAL CHART HEMISPHERES

HEMISPHERE	SIGN	AXIS	STRENGTHS
Northern	Aries x 1 Gemini x 1 Capricorn x 4 Aquarius x 2 Pisces x 1	Taurus	10

Southern	Leo x 1 Scorpio x 1 Sagittarius x 1	Scorpio	4
Western	Aries x 1 Gemini x 1 Leo x 1 Pisces x 1	Taurus	5
Eastern	Scorpio x 1 Sagittarius x 1 Capricorn x 4 Aquarius x 2	Scorpio	9

NATAL CHART QUADRANTS

You should consider the balance within your natal chart in terms of astrological quadrants as an enhancement to your self-knowledge with astrology (see Figure 67: *Natal Chart Quadrants*).

The configuration of quadrants in the natal chart example shows an emphasis on the third quadrant and the fourth quadrant with less weight on the first quadrant and the second quadrant when considering both the zodiac signs and the chart axes.

The first quadrant has been represented by the zodiac sign Leo.

The second quadrant has been represented by the zodiac signs Scorpio and Sagittarius together with Scorpio in the north node.

The third quadrant has been represented by the zodiac signs Capricorn and Aquarius.

The fourth quadrant has been represented by the zodiac signs Aries, Gemini and Pisces together with Taurus in the south node.

FIGURE 67: NATAL CHART QUADRANTS

QUADRANT	SIGN	AXIS	STRENGTHS
First	Leo x 1		1
Second	Scorpio x 1 Sagittarius x 1	Scorpio	3
Third	Capricorn x 4 Aquarius x 2		6
Fourth	Aries x 1 Gemini x 1 Pisces x 1	Taurus	4

NATAL CHART THERAPEUTIC TASKS

Consider your natal chart interpretation and the extent to which your assessment has played out in your life and within your psyche.

Evaluate the major strengths in your natal chart in terms of the sign-planet-house configurations in order to supplement your existing self-knowledge.

Evaluate the major strengths in your natal chart of the opposing zodiac signs and the astrological axes in order to gain enlightenment of your inner conflicts.

Evaluate the major strengths in your natal chart of the sign elements, sign qualities, sign genders and astrological house modes in order to deepen your self-knowledge.

Assess the entries in your natal chart in terms of astrological hemispheres and astrological quadrants in order to highlight the features of your personality and your social identity.

Undertake some meditative practice in order to contemplate the major implications in your natal chart for your life and your healing journey.

NUMEROLOGY

NUMEROLOGY

The value of numerology will be to enable you to contemplate your life's purpose and your existence in the social world.

Numerology will permit you to understand yourself and your life's mission.

NUMEROLOGICAL PRACTICE

Do you feel an affinity with the power of numbers?

Can you look at yourself as an expression of the forces of the cosmos?

Are you aware of your true nature and your natural inclinations?

WHAT IS NUMEROLOGY?

Numerology will provide you with a means of understanding yourself and your relationship with the wider world which can be interpreted via numerological data (see Figure 68: *Numerology*).

Numerology can enlighten you about your potential, talents, life purpose, motivations and character traits employing both core numbers and subsidiary numbers.

Your core numbers will comprise your life path number, your soul expression number, your soul urge number and your personality number which will influence your inner being.

Your subsidiary numbers will comprise your personal year number and your birth day number which will influence both your major life projects and your day-to-day activity.

The art of numerology was possibly first devised by Pythagoras (c569–470 BC) in ancient Greece. Pythagoras was a mathematician and a philosopher who drew on the ancient Hebrew Kabbalah and who recognised an inherent spirituality and mysticism contained within numerical data.

FIGURE 68: NUMEROLOGY

CORE NUMBERS	SUBSIDIARY NUMBERS
Life path Soul expression Soul urge Personality	Personal year Birth day

LIFE PATH NUMBERS

Are you content with your chosen mission in life?

Do you consider that you are on the path in life which best suits you?

Can you recognise the contentment which will result for you from leading a balanced existence?

WHAT IS A LIFE PATH NUMBER?

Your life path number will highlight the appropriate life mission which you might adopt.

Numbers 1 to 9 are single-digit numbers with an additional three double-digit numbers known as master numbers 11, 22 and 33. The master numbers would normally present you with some form of exacting life challenge together with the means to beneficially overcome any obstacles in order to truly fulfil your potential.

LIFE PATH NUMBER CALCULATION

You can calculate your life path number by totalling the numbers which represent your day of birth, your month of birth and your year of birth but ignoring any zeros and, when necessary, reducing the resulting number to a single-digit number or leaving your result as a double-digit master number (see Figure 69: *Life Path Number Calculation*).

FIGURE 69: LIFE PATH NUMBER CALCULATION

DATE EXAMPLE	CALCULATION	RESULT
1 January 2020	1 + 1 + 2 + 2 = 6	6
1 June 1900	1 + 6 + 1 + 9 = 17 1 + 7 = 8	8
31 December 1950	3 + 1 + 1 + 2 + 1 + 9 + 5 = 22	22

LIFE PATH NUMBER ATTRIBUTES

Once you have calculated your life path number you will be able to identify the attributes which will apply specifically to you and the direction in which you might be heading (see Figure 70: *Life Path Number Attributes*).

FIGURE 70: LIFE PATH NUMBER ATTRIBUTES

NUMBER	PATH	SYMBOLISM
1	Leader	Independent Pioneering
2	Mediator	Considerate Adaptable
3	Socialite	Expressive Jovial
4	Worker	Reliable Practical
5	Freedom lover	Adventurous Visionary
6	Peace lover	Nurturing Sympathetic
7	Thinker	Analytical Studious
8	Manager	Practical Status-seeking
9	Teacher	Humanitarian Creative
11	Giver	Generous Sensitive

22	Master builder	Ambitious Inspirational
33	Master healer	Sensitive Humble

Leader

Life path number one will be indicative of the leader who will be self-reliant, independent and pioneering in order to fulfil the life mission inherent within this number.

Mediator

Life path number two will be indicative of the mediator who will be fair-minded, considerate and adaptable in order to fulfil the life mission inherent within this number.

Socialite

Life path number three will be indicative of the socialite who will be gregarious, expressive and jovial in order to fulfil the life mission inherent within this number.

Worker

Life path number four will be indicative of the worker who will be industrious, reliable and practical in order to fulfil the life mission inherent within this number.

Freedom lover

Life path number five will be indicative of the freedom lover who will be philosophical, adventurous and visionary in order to fulfil the life mission inherent within this number.

Peace lover

Life path number six will be indicative of the peace lover who will be caring, nurturing and sympathetic in order to fulfil the life mission inherent within this number.

THINKER

Life path number seven will be indicative of the thinker who will be scholarly, analytical and studious in order to fulfil the life mission inherent within this number.

MANAGER

Life path number eight will be indicative of the manager who will be inventive, practical and status-seeking in order to fulfil the life mission inherent within this number.

TEACHER

Life path number nine will be indicative of the teacher who will be knowledgeable, humanitarian and creative in order to fulfil the life mission inherent within this number.

GIVER

Life path number eleven will be indicative of the giver who will be generous, intuitive and sensitive in order to fulfil the life mission inherent within this number.

If you are treading the giver's life path you will be presented with the challenge of realising that you do not need to prostrate yourself in the act of being generous and that you can strive for a balance of being open-hearted both to yourself and to others.

MASTER BUILDER

Life path number twenty-two will be indicative of the master builder who will be far-sighted, ambitious and inspirational in order to fulfil the life mission inherent within this number.

If you are treading the master builder's life path you will be presented with the challenge of realising that an investment in yourself will pay dividends both for yourself and for others.

MASTER HEALER

Life path number thirty-three will be indicative of the master healer who will be dedicated, spiritual and humble in order to fulfil the life mission inherent within this number.

If you are treading the master healer's life path you will be presented with the challenge of realising that there will inevitably be an imbalance in your life if you devote yourself exclusively to the service of others.

ANGELIC HEALING LINKS TO LIFE PATH NUMBERS

There are natural links from the single-digit life path numbers in numerology with angelic healing practice (see Figure 71: *Angelic Healing Links to Life Path Numbers*).

You can consider the implications of the way in which your life path mission can be assisted by your personal archangel in the therapeutic context.

FIGURE 71: ANGELIC HEALING LINKS TO LIFE PATH NUMBERS

NUMBER	PATH	ARCHANGEL
1	Leader	Raguel
2	Mediator	Uriel
3	Socialite	Jophiel
4	Worker	Haniel
5	Freedom lover	Jeremiel
6	Peace lover	Michael

7	Thinker	Raphael
8	Manager	Raziel
9	Teacher	Ariel

ASTROLOGICAL LINKS TO LIFE PATH NUMBERS

There are natural links from both the single-digit and the double-digit life path numbers in numerology with the zodiac signs and the planetary signs in astrological practice (see Figure 72: *Astrological Links to Life Path Numbers*).

You can consider the implications of the way in which your life path mission can be assisted by your personal zodiac sign and your planetary sign influences in the therapeutic context.

FIGURE 72: ASTROLOGICAL LINKS TO LIFE PATH NUMBERS

NUMBER	PATH	SIGN	PLANET
1	Leader	Leo	Sun
2	Mediator	Libra	Moon
3	Socialite	Gemini	Jupiter
4	Worker	Virgo	Uranus
5	Freedom lover	Sagittarius	Mercury
6	Peace lover	Taurus	Venus

7	Thinker	Aquarius	Neptune
8	Manager	Capricorn	Saturn
9	Teacher	Aries	Mars
11	Giver	Cancer	Sun
22	Master builder	Pisces	Moon
33	Master healer	Scorpio	Jupiter

LIFE PATH NUMBER THERAPEUTIC TASKS

Consider the nature of your life path number and its significance for you and your personal mission.

Reflect on whether you are treading the appropriate path in life in order to fulfil your true potential.

Undertake some meditative practice in order to contemplate the significance of your life path number for your life and your healing journey.

SOUL EXPRESSION NUMBERS

Do you believe that you will have little control over your destiny?

Can you acknowledge your own special skills and interests?

Could you see the way in which your personal inclinations will play out in your life?

WHAT IS A SOUL EXPRESSION NUMBER?

Your soul expression number (or destiny number) will depict the way in which your life will unfold by taking into account your skills, your talents and your interests.

SOUL EXPRESSION NUMBER CALCULATION

You can calculate your soul expression number by totalling the numbers assigned to each letter of your name according to numerology calculation practice (see Figure 73: *Soul Expression Number Calculation*).

FIGURE 73: SOUL EXPRESSION NUMBER CALCULATION

LETTER	LETTER	LETTER	NUMBER
A	J	S	1
B	K	T	2
C	L	U	3
D	M	V	4
E	N	W	5
F	O	X	6

G	P	Y	7
H	Q	Z	8
I	R		9

SOUL EXPRESSION NUMBER EXAMPLE

Your soul expression number calculation must result in a single-digit number (see Figure 74: *Soul Expression Number Example*).

FIGURE 74: SOUL EXPRESSION NUMBER EXAMPLE

NAME EXAMPLE	CALCULATION	RESULT
Santa Claus	1 + 1 + 5 + 2 + 1 + 3 + 3 + 1 + 3 + 1 = 21 2 + 1 = 3	3

SOUL EXPRESSION NUMBER ATTRIBUTES

Once you have calculated your soul expression number you will be able to identify the attributes which will apply specifically to you according to your soul expression number (see Figure 75: *Soul Expression Number Attributes*).

FIGURE 75: SOUL EXPRESSION NUMBER ATTRIBUTES

NUMBER	SYMBOLISM
1	Independence Leadership skills
2	Spiritual awareness Psychic skills

3	Creativity Inspirational skills
4	Management Organisational skills
5	Originality Innovative skills
6	Responsibility Balancing skills
7	Intellect Analytical skills
8	Security Vocational skills
9	Compassion People skills

SOUL EXPRESSION NUMBER THERAPEUTIC TASKS

Consider the nature of your soul expression number and its significance for you and your life.

Reflect on whether you feel that you are expressing yourself according to your personal inclinations rather than doing what you believe might be expected of you.

Undertake some meditative practice in order to contemplate the significance of your soul expression number for your life and your healing journey.

SOUL URGE NUMBERS

Can you pursue your personal desires without any undue hindrance?

Could you follow your heart without feeling guilty, ashamed or undeserving?

Are you able to express yourself in a creative and fulfilling manner?

WHAT IS A SOUL URGE NUMBER?

Your soul urge number (or heart's desire number) will depict the way in which you choose to creatively express yourself and to manifest your inner ideals.

SOUL URGE NUMBER CALCULATION

You can calculate your soul urge number by totalling the numbers assigned to each vowel of your name according to numerology calculation practice (see Figure 76: *Soul Urge Number Calculation*).

FIGURE 76: SOUL URGE NUMBER CALCULATION

VOWEL	NUMBER
A	1
E	5
I	9
O	6
U	3
Y	7

SOUL URGE NUMBER EXAMPLE

Your soul urge number calculation must result in a single-digit number (see Figure 77: *Soul Urge Number Example*).

FIGURE 77: SOUL URGE NUMBER EXAMPLE

NAME EXAMPLE	CALCULATION	RESULT
Romeo Montague	6 + 5 + 6 + 6 + 1 + 3 + 5 = 32 3 + 2 = 5	5

SOUL URGE NUMBER ATTRIBUTES

Once you have calculated your soul urge number you will be able to identify the attributes which will apply specifically to you according to your soul urge number (see Figure 78: *Soul Urge Number Attributes*).

FIGURE 78: SOUL URGE NUMBER ATTRIBUTES

NUMBER	SYMBOLISM
1	Successful Appreciative
2	Harmonious Diplomatic
3	Sociable Communicative
4	Secure Fulfilled
5	Free-spirited Independent
6	Acknowledging Appreciative

7	Spiritual Solitary
8	Authoritative Secure
9	Compassionate Caring

SOUL URGE NUMBER THERAPEUTIC TASKS

> Consider the nature of your soul urge number and its significance for you and your life.
>
> Reflect on whether you are following your heart in life rather than doing what you believe might be expected of you.
>
> Undertake some meditative practice in order to contemplate the significance of your soul urge number for your life and your healing journey.

PERSONALITY NUMBERS

Can you accept your personality traits as being an intrinsic part of your true nature without any apology?

Can you relish your own natural attributes and inclinations?

Are you able to put yourself at the top of your own agenda?

WHAT IS A PERSONALITY NUMBER?

Your personality number (or inner dreams number) will depict your principal character traits and your intrinsic inclinations.

PERSONALITY NUMBER CALCULATION

You can calculate your personality number by totalling the numbers assigned to each consonant of your name according to numerology calculation practice (see Figure 79: *Personality Number Calculation*).

FIGURE 79: PERSONALITY NUMBER CALCULATION

CONSONANT	CONSONANT	CONSONANT	NUMBER
J	S		1
B	K	T	2
C	L		3
D	M	V	4
N	W		5
F	X		6

G	P	Y	7
H	Q	Z	8
R			9

PERSONALITY NUMBER EXAMPLE

Your personality number calculation must result in a single-digit number (see Figure 80: *Personality Number Example*).

FIGURE 80: PERSONALITY NUMBER EXAMPLE

NAME EXAMPLE	CALCULATION	RESULT
Juliet Capulet	1 + 3 + 2 + 3 + 7 + 3 + 2 = 21 2 + 1 = 3	3

PERSONALITY NUMBER ATTRIBUTES

Once you have calculated your personality number you will be able to identify the attributes which will apply specifically to you according to your personality number (see Figure 81: *Personality Number Attributes*).

FIGURE 81: PERSONALITY NUMBER ATTRIBUTES

NUMBER	SYMBOLISM
1	Courageous Original
2	Co-operative Peaceful
3	Expressive Popular

4	Dependable Organised
5	Unrestrained Adventurous
6	Family-oriented Devoted
7	Studious Learned
8	Successful Authoritative
9	Organised Imaginative

PERSONALITY NUMBER THERAPEUTIC TASKS

> Consider the nature of your personality number and its significance for you and your life.
>
> Reflect on whether you are coming to terms with your personal inclinations and leanings rather than doing what you believe might be expected of you.
>
> Undertake some meditative practice in order to contemplate the significance of your personality number for your life and your healing journey.

PERSONAL YEAR NUMBERS

Can you identify the major projects on which you are currently engaged?

Might you see the way in which you can bring your personal desires to fruition?

Could you contemplate your actions in order to highlight your achievements?

WHAT IS A PERSONAL YEAR NUMBER?

Your personal year number will provide you with the key to the direction in which your life may be heading over a nine-year cycle for the completion of a significant project or transitory phase of your existence.

PERSONAL YEAR NUMBER CALCULATION

You can calculate your personal year number by totalling the numbers which represent your day of birth, your month of birth and the current year. Your personal year number calculation must result in a single-digit number (see Figure 82: *Personal Year Number Calculation*).

FIGURE 82: PERSONAL YEAR NUMBER CALCULATION

DATE EXAMPLE	CALCULATION	RESULT
31 December Current year 2020	3 + 1 + 1 + 2 + 2 + 2 = 11 1 + 1 = 2	2

PERSONAL YEAR NUMBER ATTRIBUTES

Once you have calculated your personal year number you will be able to identify the attributes which will apply specifically to you in your ongoing activities and projects according to your personal year number (see Figure 83: *Personal Year Number Attributes*).

FIGURE 83: PERSONAL YEAR NUMBER ATTRIBUTES

NUMBER	SYMBOLISM
1	Action
2	Companionship
3	Sociability
4	Development
5	Exploration
6	Contentment
7	Reflection
8	Accomplishment
9	Completion

PERSONAL YEAR NUMBER THERAPEUTIC TASKS

Consider the nature of your personal year number and its significance for you and your life.

Reflect on your personal year number and estimate where your life might currently be heading.

Undertake some meditative practice in order to contemplate the significance of your personal year number for your life and your healing journey.

BIRTH DAY NUMBERS

Do you recognise and applaud the person you really are?

Can you capitalise on your personal attributes and exploit your talents to the full?

Do you understand yourself as well as comprehending other people?

WHAT IS A BIRTH DAY NUMBER?

Your birth day number will provide you with the key to your talents and your unique personal attributes which will assist you throughout life.

BIRTH DAY NUMBER CALCULATION

You can calculate your birth day number by considering the day of the month in which you were born. Your birth day number calculation must result in a single-digit number (see Figure 84: *Birth Day Number Calculation*).

FIGURE 84: BIRTH DAY NUMBER CALCULATION

DATE EXAMPLE	CALCULATION	RESULT
Birth date 21	2 + 1 = 3	3

BIRTH DAY NUMBER ATTRIBUTES

Once you have calculated your birth day number you will be able to identify the attributes which will apply specifically to you and your existence according to your birth day number (see Figure 85: *Birth Day Number Attributes*).

FIGURE 85: BIRTH DAY NUMBER ATTRIBUTES

DAY	SYMBOLISM
1 and 28	Leadership-oriented Original-thinking

2	Sensitive Sociable
3, 12 and 21	Determined Resilient
4	Responsible Self-disciplined
5, 14 and 23	Gregarious Versatile
6	Helpful Understanding
7 and 25	Individualistic Analytical
8 and 26	Entrepreneurial Reliable
9 and 27	Idealistic Philanthropic
10	Independent Self-confident
11	Dreamy Spiritual
13	Managerial Organised
15	Family-oriented Capable
16	Flexible Independent

17	Ethical Shrewd
18	Humanitarian Broad-minded
19	Energetic Powerful
20	Psychic Intuitive
22	Steadfast Far-sighted
24	Humanitarian Considerate
29	Imaginative Creative
30	Free-thinking Self-expressive
31	Sincere Patient

BIRTH DAY NUMBER THERAPEUTIC TASKS

Consider the nature of your birth day number and its significance for you and your life.

Reflect on whether you are expressing those personal attributes which are related to your birth day number.

Undertake some meditative practice in order to contemplate the significance of your birth day number for your life and your healing journey.

HEALING RAYS

HEALING RAYS

The value of the healing rays will be to enlighten you about your place in the world.

The healing rays will permit you to understand the way in which your personal interests and your occupational inclinations will assist you with your healing journey.

HEALING RAY PRACTICE

Might you be aware that you can heal yourself in a number of different ways?

Can you acknowledge that your work and your leisure both serve a useful purpose for you?

Are you able to balance your work and your play effectively?

WHAT IS A HEALING RAY?

The seven healing rays will be beams of coloured vibrational energy which will provide you with a means of self-evolution through everyday activity within your normal sphere of life (see Figure 86: *Healing Rays*).

FIGURE 86: HEALING RAYS

Colour	Number
Blue	First
Yellow	Second
Pink	Third
White	Fourth
Green	Fifth
Purple	Sixth
Violet	Seventh

HEALING RAY LIFE PATH

Are you a scientist or an artist by nature or anything in between?

Do you seek to help others as a means of helping yourself?

Can you appreciate yourself as a fully rounded personality?

WHAT IS A HEALING RAY LIFE PATH?

The healing rays will represent the choices which you will make in your life about your profession, your leisure pursuits and your social life and these decisions will assist your healing journey particularly when you derive pleasure and satisfaction from undertaking these activities (see Figure 87: *Healing Ray Paths*).

Your adoption of the life path of one or more of the healing rays will allow you to engage in activity in a meaningful way, to pursue your dearest interests and to develop your talents according to your personal preferences. When you can identify your mission in life in a number of spheres and you can fulfil your true potential in these areas you will then naturally be on a healing path for yourself.

Your healing ray paths will allow you to attain greater self-satisfaction and contentment rather than doing what you feel you ought to do or you believe you are obliged to do.

FIGURE 87: HEALING RAY PATHS

RAY	SYMBOLISM	OCCUPATION
Blue	Willpower Initiative	Explorer Manager Politician
Yellow	Love Unification	Healer Philanthropist Teacher

Pink	Intelligence Evolution	Economist Historian Philosopher
White	Harmony Self-knowledge	Artist Musician Therapist
Green	Science Action	Engineer Researcher Scientist
Purple	Idealism Philanthropy	Minister Missionary Orator
Violet	Order Self-expression	Administrator Builder Designer

BLUE RAY

The blue ray will be the first healing ray which will govern your willpower, energy and drive. When you adopt the blue ray as your healing ray you may be drawn to being self-motivated and able to initiate new ventures and enterprises for yourself.

YELLOW RAY

The yellow ray will be the second healing ray which will govern your intimate relationships and your relationship with yourself. When you adopt the yellow ray as your healing ray you may be drawn to uniting groups and bringing people together as well as loving and respecting yourself.

PINK RAY

The pink ray will be the third healing ray which will govern your intelligence, academic aptitudes and communication ability. When you adopt the pink ray as your healing ray you may be drawn to academic study, debate and philosophical reasoning.

White ray

The white ray will be the fourth healing ray which will govern your creativity and artistic abilities. When you adopt the white ray as your healing ray you may be drawn to artistic endeavour and your consequent self-development through your creativity.

Green ray

The green ray will be the fifth healing ray which will govern your scientific experimentation and research interests. When you adopt the green ray as your healing ray you may be drawn to investigation and discovery in order to augment your knowledge-base.

Purple ray

The purple ray will be the sixth healing ray which will govern your idealism, integrity and life purpose. When you adopt the purple ray as your healing ray you may be drawn to supporting worthy causes and devoting your life to the service of mankind.

Violet ray

The violet ray will be the seventh healing ray which will govern your planning ability, design conceptualisation and constructive aims. When you adopt the violet ray as your healing ray you may be drawn to being methodical and organised in order to achieve tangible results.

Energetic healing links to healing rays

The healing rays can be utilised in conjunction with physiological and psychological healing via the lower chakra system and the endocrine system (see Figure 88: *Energetic Healing Links to Healing Rays*).

You can invoke the power of the healing rays as related to specific parts your physical system which will require special attention during your healing practice. The healing rays do not, of course, correspond to the vibrational colours normally associated with the chakra systems.

FIGURE 88: ENERGETIC HEALING LINKS TO HEALING RAYS

RAY	CHAKRA	HUMAN SYSTEM
Blue	Crown	Pineal
Yellow	Heart	Thymus
Pink	Throat	Thyroid
White	Base	Adrenals
Green	Anya	Pituitary
Purple	Solar Plexus	Pancreas
Violet	Sacral	Gonads

ANGELIC HEALING LINKS TO HEALING RAYS

The healing rays will be associated with the archangels and the ascended masters of angelic healing practice in order to assist you to fulfil your life's mission and to attain peace and contentment (see Figure 89: *Angelic Healing Links to Healing Rays*).

You can invoke the power of the archangels and the ascended masters in order to assist you with self-healing via the healing rays.

FIGURE 89: ANGELIC HEALING LINKS TO HEALING RAYS

RAY	ARCHANGEL	ASCENDED MASTER
Blue	Michael	El Morya Khan

Yellow	Jophiel	Lord Lanto
Pink	Chamuel	Paul the Venetian
White	Gabriel	Serapis Bay
Green	Raphael	Hilarion
Purple	Uriel	Lady Nada
Violet	Zadkiel	Saint Germain

ASTROLOGICAL LINKS TO HEALING RAYS

Each healing ray will be linked to three zodiac signs and one or more planetary signs which will outline your life's mission and your personal preferences in accordance with esoteric astrology (see Figure 90: *Astrological Links to Healing Rays*).

These healing ray links with esoteric astrology will help you to understand yourself and your mission in life in order to allow you to progress through your self-development.

FIGURE 90: ASTROLOGICAL LINKS TO HEALING RAYS

RAY	SYMBOLISM	SIGN	PLANET
Blue	Willpower	Aries Leo Capricorn	Pluto Vulcan
Yellow	Love	Gemini Virgo Pisces	Sun Jupiter

Pink	Intelligence	Cancer Libra Capricorn	Saturn Earth
White	Harmony	Taurus Scorpio Sagittarius	Moon Mercury
Green	Science	Leo Sagittarius Aquarius	Venus
Purple	Idealism	Virgo Sagittarius Pisces	Mars Neptune
Violet	Order	Aries Cancer Capricorn	Uranus

HEALING RAYS THERAPEUTIC TASKS

Consider the importance of the seven healing rays which are the most relevant and appropriate for you.

Reflect on the significance of your chosen healing rays as they affect your current existence and estimate the way in which you can further your healing journey accordingly.

Undertake some meditative practice in order to contemplate the major implications of your healing rays and their links to energetic healing and angelic healing.

Undertake some meditative practice in order to contemplate the major implications of your healing rays and their links to the zodiac signs and the planetary signs in your natal chart.

APPENDICES

FURTHER READING

A Guide to Energetic Healing: From Clearing Trauma/Abuse to Raising Consciousness – John Nelson (Rainbow Ridge Books)

Analytical Hypnotherapy: Practical Applications – Jacquelyne Morison (Crown House Publishing)

Analytical Hypnotherapy: Theoretical Principals – Jacquelyne Morison (Crown House Publishing)

Analytical Psychology: Its Theory and Practice – Carl Jung (Routledge)

Angelic Healing: Change your Life with Help from the Angels – Jenny Smedley (CICO Books)

Astrology for the Soul – Jan Spiller (Bantam Books)

Creative Analytical Hypnotherapy: The Practitioner's Handbook – Jacquelyne Morison (Jacquelyne Morison Publishing)

Esoteric Astrology – Alice Bailey (Lucis Press Ltd)

Esoteric Astrology: A New Astrology for a New Millennium – Douglas Baker (Baker Publications)

Hands of Light: Guide to Healing Through the Human Energy Field – Barbara Ann Brennan (Bantam)

Healing the Soul: Pluto, Uranus and the Lunar Nodes – Mark Jones (Raven Dreams Publications)

Natural Law in the Spiritual World – Henry Drummond (Create Space Independent Publishing Platform)

North Node Astrology: Rediscovering Your Life Direction and Soul Purpose – Elizabeth Spring (Archaeon Press)

Presence in Relationship: Offering Core Process Psychotherapy – Susan Groves (Create Space independent Publishing Platform)

Psychosynthesis Counselling in Action – Diana Whitmore (Sage Publications)

Psychotherapy and Spirit: Theory and Practice in Transpersonal Psychotherapy – Brant Cortright (State University of New York Press)

Shamanic Healing: Traditional Medicine for the Modern World – Itzhak Beery (Destiny Books)

Spiritual Accompaniment and Counselling: Journeying with Psyche and Soul – Peter Madsen (Jessica Kingsley Publishers)

Spiritual Healing: A Beginners Guide – Lois Hewitt (Create Space Independent Publishing Platform)

Spiritual Healing: Expanded Edition – Robert E Detzler (SCR Publishing)

Spiritual Laws that Govern Humanity and the Universe – Lonnie C Edwards (Rosicrucian Order)

The Book of Shamanic Healing – Kristin Madden (Llewellyn Publications)

The Everything Guide to Angels: Discover the Wisdom and Healing Power of the Angelic Kingdom – Karen Paulino (Adams Media)

The Seven Rays of Life – Alice Bailey (Lucis Press Ltd)

The Shamanic Journey: A Practical Guide to Therapeutic Shamanism – Paul Frances (Paul Frances)

The Soul of Psychosynthesis: The Seven Core Concepts – Kenneth Sørenson (Kentaur Publishing)

The Transpersonal: Spirituality in Psychotherapy and Counselling – John Rowan (Routledge)

Transpersonal Psychotherapy: Theory and Practice – Nigel Wellings and Elizabeth Wilde McCormick (Sage Publications)

Unfolding Self: The Practice of Psychosynthesis – Molly Young Brown (Allworth Press)

INDEX

Adulthood, 12, 94, 102, 151
Age of Aquarius, 121
Age of Pisces, 120
Age-regression, 55
Akashic records, 69, 83
Alternative therapy, 26, 36
Archetypal symbolism, 3, 4
Assagioli, Robert, 7
Battista, John, 6
Career path, 14
Cerebral cortex, 38
Character analysis, 3
Chi, 36, 38
Childhood, 13, 15, 25, 61, 102, 150
Clairaudience, 57
Clairsentience, 57
Clairvoyance, 25, 38, 51, 57
Colour healing, 3
Complementary medicine, 36
Confidence, 13, 14, 21, 22, 82
Creative visualisation, 4, 5, 23, 36, 39
Crystal healing, 3
Divination, 4, 101
Dream symbolism, 6
Electro-magnetic fields, 37

Endocrine system, 37, 45, 47, 50
Family, 17, 19, 29, 61, 136, 141
Great spirit, 38
Grof, Stanislav, 6
Healing mission, 18, 52, 73, 75, 85
Herbalism, 36
Holistic healing, 36
Humanistic psychotherapy, 6, 7
Hypnotic state, 91, 92
Immune system, 48, 49
Individuation, 7
Intuition, 25, 51, 53, 54, 103, 109, 124, 131, 137, 141, 143, 146
Jung, Carl, 6, 203
Kabbalah, 169
Life partner, 13, 14, 16
Limbic system, 39, 45
Lunar nodes, 151
Massage, 36
Meditation, 4, 22, 23
Meridian channels, 37
Mindfulness, 7
Motivation, 13, 17, 38, 57, 80, 83, 86, 108, 111, 139, 152
Music-sound healing, 3

Native American medicine, 93
Nutritional medicine, 36
Past-life regression, 36, 55
Philosophy, 3, 45, 83, 94, 120, 121
Prana, 38
Psyche, 23, 26, 82, 96, 101, 106, 119, 148, 149, 150, 151, 156
Psychodynamic psychotherapy, 6, 7
Pythagoras, 169
Reiki healing, 3, 35
Reincarnation, 39
Relaxation, 4, 23, 60
Security, 17, 108, 125, 135, 140, 142, 145, 182
Self-concept, 69, 80
Self-discovery, 56
Self-empowerment, 48
Self-enlightenment, 82, 92
Self-healing, 16, 23, 25, 26, 27, 35, 36, 42, 56, 77, 81, 85, 146
Self-hypnosis, 5, 22, 36
Self-image, 49, 69
Shaman, 91
Sills, Maura, 7
Society, 10, 17, 50, 96, 127
Spirit guides, 69, 72, 93, 97
Spiritual healing, 35
Transcendence, 6
Transpersonal psychotherapy, 6
Vaughan, Frances, 6
Vibrational medicine, 36
Vortex healing, 3, 35
Walsh, Roger, 6
Washburn, Michael, 6
Wealth, 17, 18, 26, 108, 112, 123, 125, 126, 140
Wilber, Ken, 6

ABOUT JACQUELYNE MORISON

Jacquelyne Morison is the founder and course director of Jacquelyne Morison Hypnotherapy Training.

Jacquelyne Morison Hypnotherapy Training provides hypnotherapy training courses for both prospective practitioners and working professionals (www.jmhypnotraining.co.uk).

Jacquelyne Morison Hypnotherapy Training also runs practitioner-level courses for prospective practitioners of Psycho-Spiritual Therapy.

Jacquelyne is the author of *Hypnotherapy Teaching, Training and Supervision*, *Creative Analytical Hypnotherapy*, *Analytical Hypnotherapy Volumes 1-2*, *The Truly Dynamic Therapist* and *Hypnotic Art Therapy*. She is also a chapter contributor to *Clinical Hypnosis Textbook: A Guide to Practical Intervention* by Ursula James.

Jacquelyne holds a Bachelor of Arts (BA) honours degree in Clinical Hypnosis and a Post-Graduate Certificate in Education (PGCE) for Post-Compulsory Education and Training. Jacquelyne also holds a Master of Arts (MA) degree in music and a Bachelor of Music (BMus) honours degree.

Prior to entering the therapeutic profession Jacquelyne was formerly a Business Studies Teacher, an IT Training Consultant and a Technical Author.

www.ingramcontent.com/pod-product-compliance
Lightning Source LLC
Chambersburg PA
CBHW061141010526
44118CB00026B/2840